The Authentic Guide to DRINKS OF THE CIVIL WAR ERA

1853 - 1873

Sharon Peregrine Johnson
&
Byron A. Johnson

THOMAS PUBLICATIONS
Gettysburg PA 17325

Printed in the United States of America

Published by THOMAS PUBLICATIONS
       P.O. Box 3031
       Gettysburg, PA 17325

ISBN-0-939631-45-8

Cover design by Ryan C. Stouch. Front cover photograph, "Here's to the gal I
love," courtesy of William Welling (see also pages 67, 145, 152 and 200). Back
cover photograph of an unidentified Federal sergeant courtesy of Philip Katcher
and the David Scheinmann Collection.

To Carmen Martin
and
the New Mexico Civil War Commemorative Congress

Contents

Scotch Whiskey (About 10 Gallons)
Bordeaux Wine (About 10 Gallons) Red
Bordeaux Wine (About 10 Gallons) White
Champagne (About 10 Gallons)

A Humbug and a Nuisance as Regards Health *153*

Cheap Ale
Cheap Porter for Bottling
Apple Brandy (About 40 Gallons)
Cognac Brandy (About 112 Gallons)
Cognac Brandy (5 Gallons)
Cognac Brandy (5 Gallons)
New York Brandy (About 72 Gallons)
Peach Brandy (130 Gallons)
English Gin (About 108 Gallons)
Holland Gin (5 Gallons)
Holland Gin (100 Gallons)
New York Gin (100 Gallons)
Cheap New York Gin (100 Gallons)
Rose Gin (100 Gallons)
Schiedam Schnapps Gin—Aromatic (About 4 Gallons)
Schiedam Swan Gin (100 Gallons)
Jamaica Rum (About 5 Gallons)
Jamaica Rum (About 122 Gallons)
St. Croix Rum (About 110 Gallons)
Old Bourbon Whiskey (5 Gallons)
Old Bourbon Whiskey (126 Gallons)
Old Bourbon Whiskey for Bottling (About 7 Gallons)
Irish Whiskey (133 Gallons)
Cheap Irish Whiskey (About 30 Gallons)
Monongahela Whiskey (5 Gallons)
Monongahela Whiskey (About 128 Gallons)
Monongahela Whiskey for Bottling (About 6 Gallons)
Monongahela Rye Whiskey (About 123 Gallons)
Old Roanoke Whiskey (About 40 Gallons)
Old Rye Whiskey (5 Gallons)
Old Rye Whiskey (About 125 Gallons)
Scotch Whiskey (About 136 Gallons)

Preface

This work contains 263 recipes carefully selected from rare bartenders', distillers', and "liquorists'" guidebooks published between 1853 and 1873. It is intended to assist Civil War enthusiasts and reenactors in mixing the authentic drinks and punches of the era.

Facsimiles of 19th century cookbooks have been available for some time, but there has been little available on the popular libations consumed in taverns, military camps and homes. Few now realize that mixed drinks were as popular as straight liquor, or that real Southern mint juleps of the 1850s and 1860s were made with fine Cognac, not Bourbon.

To use this book, please begin with the chapter "The Civil War Sideboard." It lists modern conversions for such arcane 1860s measurements as "wine glass," "pony" and "champagne glass." The chapter also contains a roster of liquors and ingredients that will enable ambitious imbibers to stock a Civil War tavern, or recreate the liquor cabinet of a well to do 1860s family. Less determined readers may simply wish to make a list of the liquors and ingredients in the drinks that appeal to them.

The first 208 recipes are for mixed drinks and punches that can be safely prepared and enjoyed today. After more than 130 years, most of the liquors, liqueurs (cordials), syrups, and other ingredients of the 1860s are still available at better liquor stores, gourmet shops, and delicatessens. If you shop carefully, it is possible to use many liquors that are essentially unchanged since the Civil War era.

For example, General Grant was fond of Old Crow Bourbon Whiskey—still commonly available. Wealthy Confederates imported Glenlivet whiskey in the holds of blockade runners. It is essentially the same Glenlivet available at the corner liquor store. The brand Triple Sec is essentially the same as the greatly favored 19th century liqueur Curacao. The Glossary describes each liquor or ingredient and provides substitutes for those no longer available.

Liqueurs (cordials) and fruit brandies are essential to many drinks of the Civil War era. Wherever possible, try to use "true fruit" instead of artificially flavored liqueurs and brandies. Fruit brandies of the 1860s were made from the distilled mash (pulp) of fermented fruit. Liqueurs (cordials) usually consisted of grain alcohol or grape brandy flavored with real spices, herbs and fruit extracts.

Most of the cheap liqueurs and fruit brandies now lining the shelves of liquor stores are made from modern synthetic flavorings and grain alcohol. Stay away from them if authenticity is your goal. They provide quick intoxication, but they are an atrocious substitute for real fruit brandies and liqueurs. In some cases you may have to seek out more expensive European "true fruit" liqueurs at better liquor stores. But you will be able to taste the difference.

There has been much speculation about how liquors were diluted, or what went into the bogus imitation liquors foisted on soldiers during the war. In the chapter "The Manufacture of Liquors" we have included a dozen recipes illustrating common methods of diluting liquors and manufacturing "safe" imitations. While we cannot recommend watering down good liquors, or making your own rum or ale, these recipes are safer than the completely spurious products of the 1860s.

The chapter "A Humbug and a Nuisance to the Health" contains 37 recipes for "sutlers' poisons"—the infamous counterfeit liquors that contained such ingredients as impure grain alcohol, toxic chemicals, peppers, acids, dyes and ethers. They are included only for historical interest. Please do not attempt to make or consume any of these beverages. Mixing acids and ethers can cause burns or property damage. Consumption could lead to serious internal injuries or death. They are included solely to illustrate the type of noxious potions dishonest sutlers and war profiteers passed off as genuine liquors.

The majority of the recipes are quoted as they were originally written to preserve the literary style of the period. We have edited them only when necessary for clarity.

As with any alcoholic beverages, please drink moderately and at the right times. Don't drink when riding, employing artillery, engaging enemy troops, or in proximity to muskets, pistols or camp followers. Thanks.

Sharon Peregrine Johnson
Byron A. Johnson
Rio Rancho, New Mexico

Introduction

In the *Social History of Bourbon*, Gerald Carson wrote "In troubled times men seek the solace of religion or strong drink, or both." During the dark days of the Civil War, soldiers, politicians and civilians alike sought escape and relaxation in spirituous refreshments.

Towns like Washington and Richmond were full of taverns and hotel bars where politicians and spies plotted strategy and intrigue over straight and mixed drinks. Contrary to modern belief, mixed drinks—with sweeteners, bitters, spices, fruits, herbs and liqueurs—were as popular as straight drinks. Many of these mixed drinks were of English, Irish and German derivation, as befitted a nation of immigrants. Others were purely "American sensations," fad drinks popular enough to lead "peripatetic Americans" to set up English pubs that served what one writer described as "Connecticut eye-openers, Alabama fog-cutters, lightning-smashes and thunderbolt- cocktails." Unlike the modern penchant for "dry" drinks, these beverages were usually sweetened with large amounts of syrups and sugar.

It was also the age of punch. Loved ones at home and soldiers on leave concocted a bewildering variety of punch bowl drinks for holidays, cotillions and reunions. Their "flowing bowls" ran with concoctions such as *Spread Eagle Punch* (see #181), *Bimbo Punch* (see #121), *National Guard Seventh Regiment Punch* (see #157) and *A Splitting Headache* (see #188). Some of these mixtures featured ten or more liquors, cordials, syrups, bitters and fruits.

There was abundant drinking among Union and Confederate armies in the field. Officers realized that a conservative ration of spirits could revive tired and demoralized soldiers. Early in the war, Union officers were authorized to issue daily quarter pint rations of whiskey to each man. Unfortunately, as the war lengthened, officers and enlisted men drank to excess more frequently to escape the horrors and monotony of war.

Drunkenness became a serious threat to readiness as the war continued. General George McClellan declared that nothing was as damaging to the war effort "as the degrading vice of drunkenness." He felt that its eradication would be the equivalent of adding 50,000 troops to the Union army. CSA General Braxton Bragg lamented that the South had "lost more valuable lives at the hands of the whiskey sellers than by the [musket] balls of our enemies."

Confederate commanders appear to have been more tolerant of drinking than their Union counterparts. Photographs verify that jugs and demijohns (large wicker-covered bottles) were common around Confederate camps early in the war. As the conflict lengthened, and food became scarce in the South, the Confederacy passed laws prohibiting the distillation of liquor from cereal grains, potatoes and fruits. The price of quality blended whiskey in the Confederacy rose from twenty-five cents per gallon in 1861 to twenty-five dollars per gallon in 1863.

Both Northern and Southern officers decried the effects of alcohol on their troops. Long dry spells, followed by binges on liquor of dubious composition, left soldiers too debilitated for battle. As restrictions on drinking became more severe, enlisted men became more inventive, smuggling liquor into camp in secreted flasks and bottles or poured into their rifle barrels. Mail order books contained instructions on how to make real or imitation brandy, whiskey, gin, rum, beer, ale and wine. Enterprising soldiers concealed makeshift stills and breweries in both Union and Confederate winter camps. Any foodstuff that would ferment was employed.

An examination of recipes for homemade and imitation liquors leads to an interesting question: were the binges of enlisted men and noncommissioned officers that bad, or was the quality of the liquor worse? Official Union whiskey rations came from army commissaries supplied by government contractors. Early in the war Union enlisted men drew their whiskey rations from these stocks. After the official whiskey ration was cancelled, commissary whiskey was sold only to officers at prices ranging around thirty cents a gallon. Routine inspections ensured that commissary whiskey was rarely poisonous in reasonable quantities. Nonetheless, it was famous for being poorly distilled, unpalatably "green" (poorly aged) and often "BP" (below proof, meaning weak or diluted).

Enlisted men on both sides of the conflict usually purchased their liquor from camp sutlers. Officially, these mobile merchants were often forbidden to trade in alcoholic beverages, but most did a thriving business as bootleggers. The usual beverage was labeled "whiskey," but on occasion they stocked "gin," "brandy," "rum" or "high wines."

A few sutlers were honest men who sold quality liquors. Others, perhaps the majority, belonged to a "wretched class of swindlers" who sold poisonous compounds that could produce more trauma than enemy fire. One often-quoted Indiana officer declared that his liquor was made of "bark juice, tar-water, brown sugar, lamp-oil and alcohol." While his statement may have been written tongue-in-cheek, recipes for fake liquors of the period did call for such ingredients as sulfuric acid, creosote, vinegar, nitric and acetic ether, astringents and extract of Guinea (West African) pepper.

A Few Words About Sources. . .

The primary sources for this guide book are rare saloonkeepers', brewers' and distillers' guides published between 1853 and 1873. Between 1860 and 1900 more than 150,000 persons entered the liquor trade in the U.S. Keeping a tavern or saloon was hailed as a means of upward mobility for native born Americans and waves of English, Irish and German immigrants. The burgeoning tavern-keeping profession created a large market for instructional literature on how to mix drinks, distill liquors and cordials, and brew beer and ale.

Six manuals made it possible to compile this work. The most important to an understanding of the drinks of the Civil War era is *How to Mix Drinks*, or the *Bon-Vivant's Companion* (New York: Dick and Fitzgerald, 1862) written by Jeremiah "Jerry" Thomas.

Jerry Thomas, author of How to Mix Drinks *or* Bon-Vivant's Companion, *ensconced in his New York saloon about 1880.*

Although he is now almost forgotten, and usually uncredited in modern bar books, "Professor" Jerry Thomas was the dean of 19th century bartenders. Contemporaries said that his name was "synonymous in the lexicon of mixed drinks, with all that is rare and original." They called him the "Jupiter Olympus," and "presiding deity" of any bar he tended.

Although details regarding his life are scarce, and many are suspect, we do know that Jerry Thomas was born in New Haven, Connecticut in 1825. His English-born parents intended for him to be a minister, but at twenty Jerry apprenticed as an assistant to the principal bartender of a New Haven tavern. He learned the trade just as the 19th saloon was evolving in form from the colonial tavern to the saloon of America's Gilded Age.

Young Jerry learned his trade in an 1840s barroom that was nearly indistinguishable from a 1740s tavern. Customers called for their alcoholic refreshments at a counter and drank them with friends at tables, much the same as when Connecticut was an English colony. Customers knew each other, and they could mark the passage of the seasons by the availability of hot and cold beverages.

The first drinks that Apprentice Tavern-keeper Thomas served were British and German beverages: ale and beer mixtures, cups, flips, mulls, noggs, bowls, negus, shrubs, and mixed drinks based on brandies, port and Madeira. Hot and cold punch bowl drinks were especially popular. Tavern drinking was a rite of passage and an important social activity for the leaders of the community. The founding fathers of the previous century, such as John Adams or Thomas Jefferson, would have been quite at home in Thomas' New Haven tavern.

When gold was discovered in California, thousands of would-be miners, prospectors and businessmen, including Jerry Thomas, booked passage and sailed for the Pacific Coast. Twenty-four year old Thomas arrived in San Francisco harbor in 1849 aboard the bark *Annie Smith*. He soon secured a position as First Assistant to the Principal Bartender of the El Dorado saloon.

Jerry quickly became a celebrity at the El Dorado. The customers of the saloon were "rough characters" from the

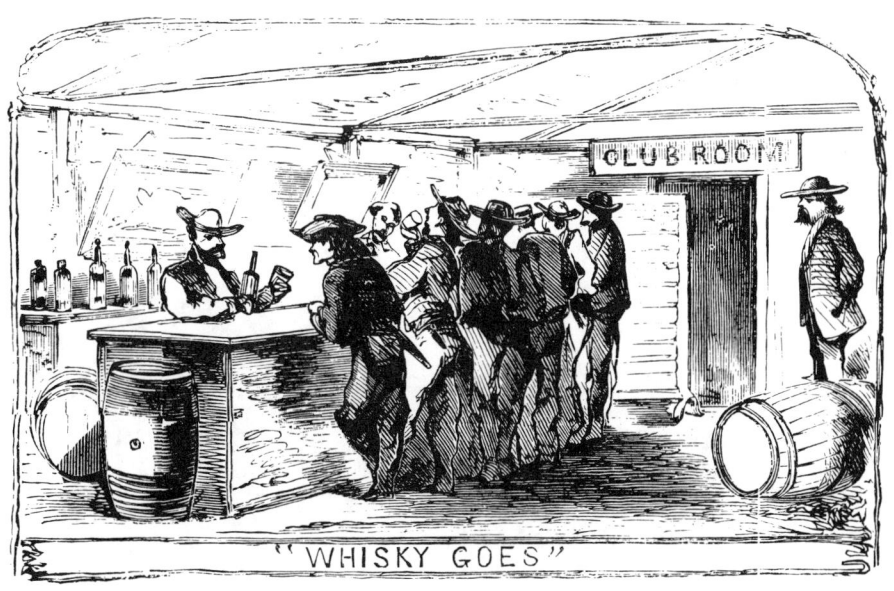

Tent saloons, similar to this 1869 example, were hastily set up around military encampments. They were also common in border areas like Kansas and Missouri.

placers, mines and the waterfront, men who drank for sheer effect. Only whiskeys, brandies and inferior local beer were available to saloon patrons for the first few months of the Gold Rush. Few ships brought supplies to San Francisco; it was far more profitable to haul prospectors than merchandise. The limited selection of liquors quickly became tedious. Bartenders endeavored to relieve the boredom of their customers by improvising potent drinks, yielding dramatic effects, with what was on hand.

It was during this time that Thomas allegedly invented the *Blue Blazer* (see #48), to please a miner who wanted something that would "shake him down to his gizzard." He filled a pewter mug with half 90 proof whiskey and half boiling water, set it on fire, and poured it into another mug. In the dim, whale oil lit saloon the mixture looked like a continual stream of liquid fire as he poured it back and forth. According to legend, the miner was so delighted with the drink that he presented Thomas with two ounces of gold nuggets. The famous Blue Blazer is mostly showmanship; much of the alcohol is consumed by the flame. Supply ships eventually arrived carrying a wide variety of American and European fruit brandies, cordials, exotic liquors, bitters and garnishes.

A common practice in many saloons was the free oyster with every drink.

John Austin, principal bartender of Meagher's Saloon in New York. Principal bartenders of the 1860s often wore expensive dress suits while their assistants dressed in white linen or cotton jackets.

About 1851 Thomas left San Francisco for the Yuba City gold fields to become principal bartender for a Donaville saloon. He quickly accumulated a $16,000 fortune by working in the gold fields during the day and tending bar at night. With fortune in hand, Thomas boarded a ship bound for New York and then headed back to New Haven.

Unable to find happiness in Connecticut, Thomas wandered from 1854 until 1865. He allegedly accepted bartending positions in South Carolina, Chicago, at the Planter's House in St. Louis, at the bar of the Metropolitan Hotel in New York, and various bars in New Orleans.

Thomas' stint in New Orleans resulted in a friendship with Santina, the owner of a Spanish style cafe-saloon, who allegedly invented the Crusta and popularized the multilayered Pousse Cafe. After this he journeyed abroad to Liverpool, London, and Paris. He returned to California during the early 1860s and remained there until the war ended in 1865.

Everywhere Thomas went he picked up new recipes or modified old ones according to the tastes of his customers. At the Planter's House in St. Louis he modified an old Danish punch bowl drink, the *Copenhagen*, and created the *Tom and Jerry* (see #186). Authorities have argued that the name of this drink is a corruption of his name, Jerry Thomas, but there is evidence that the name *Tom and Jerry* was applied to other drinks before Thomas' mixture.

"Professor" Thomas, as he was called, barnstormed around the country giving public demonstrations of his mixological prowess, aided by a custom made $4,000 set of solid silver bartending utensils. He eventually settled in New York where he owned several saloons. The idea for Thomas' bar book originated about 1860 when a principal of the publishing firm of Dick and Fitzgerald went to London:

> We very well remember seeing one day in London, in the rear of the Bank of England, a small drinking saloon that had been set up by a peripatetic American, at the door of which was placed a board covered with the unique titles of the American mixed drinks supposed to be prepared within that limited establishment. [These drinks] created a profound sensation in the crowd assembled to peruse the Nectarian bill of fare, if they did not produce custom.
>
> It struck us, then, that a list of all the social drinks—the composite beverages, if we may call them so—of America, would really be one of the curiosities of jovial literature; and that if it was combined with a catalogue of the mixtures common to other nations, and made practically useful by the addition of a concise description of the various processes for 'brewing' each, it would be a 'blessing to mankind.' There would be no excuse for imbibing, with such a book at hand, the 'villainous compounds' of barkeeping Goths and Vandals, who know no more of the amenities of bon vivant existence than a Hottentot can know of the bouquet of champagne.

No one knew more about mixed drinks than Jerry Thomas, and Dick and Fitzgerald persuaded him to write the book. In actuality, it is likely that he merely organized and converted his personal notes into a readable form with the help of an editor. The first edition was published as *How to Mix Drinks*, or the *Bon-Vivant's Companion* (New York: Dick and Fitzgerald, 1862) for professional and amateur mixologists. It quickly became the

MAIN STREET

The tent and shack towns typical of border states and territories featured several saloons per block.

Bible of bartending; at least eleven editions were printed between 1862 and 1934. Probably written in California, and published in the midst of the Civil War, Thomas' book is a wonderful compendium of drinks of the time.

Newsstands and book stores from California to New York carried the *Bon-Vivant's Companion*. Every earnest saloon and hotel bar had a copy of Jerry's work beneath the bar. To this day Thomas' book ranks second only to the *Mr. Boston Official Bartender's Guide* in number of editions printed.

Bound together with Thomas' book was an equally valuable treatise by Christian Schultz, *Manual for the Manufacture of Cordials, Liquors, Fancy Syrups, &c. &c.* (New York: Dick and Fitzgerald, 1862). We know little about Schultz other than the fact that he claimed to be a native of Bern, Switzerland, and a professor of chemistry and apothecary. Schultz provided instructions and diagrams on how to construct a still and a filtration apparatus, as well as recipes for the manufacture of more than 400 syrups, cordials and liquors. Unlike his contemporary, Pierre Lacour of New Orleans, Schultz' products were safe to drink and use. One could become a professional or home bartender with little more than the Thomas/Schultz book.

In direct contrast to Thomas' and Schultz' sound advice was Pierre Lacour's *The Manufacture of Liquors, Wines, and Cordials,*

Charley McCarty, principal bartender of the St. James Hotel.

Without the Aid of Distillation, (New York: Dick and Fitzgerald, 1853). Lacour was a native of Bordeaux who resided among the expatriate French in New Orleans. His book was a thieves' and poisoner's guide to the manufacture of imitation liquors.

Lacour advised his readers on how to use poor quality grain alcohol, acids, creosote, pepper, ether, astringents, ground isinglass, ammonia and other ingredients to make whiskey, champagne and high wines. Some evidence suggests that Lacour's guide became a best seller among unethical sutlers and liquor sellers of the period. Lacour also instructed his readers in how to make fake wine, beer and ale, obtain false bottle labels from printers, and sell their wares at auctions (presumably so they could not be traced.)

Several other books were of great assistance in understanding the drinks of the period:

Edward Ricket's *The Gentleman's Table Guide and Table Companion* (London: F. Warne, 1873) is a proper Victorian Englishman's guide to setting a proper table. It contains recipes for traditional English, Irish, Scottish and German drinks as well as a selection of American drinks collected by Ricket in the 1860s.

George Edwin Roberts' *Cups and Their Customs* (London: John Van Voorst, 1863, 1869) is a rambling essay full of traditional English recipes for punch bowl drinks (cups). Soldiers of English extraction would have been very familiar with the beverages cited by Roberts.

Leonard Monzert's *The Independent Liquorist* (New York: Dick and Fitzgerald, n.d., c1866) is a guide to bartending and the operation of a wholesale liquor establishment.

Stocking a Civil War Sideboard

The following conversion chart will aid in mixing the drinks of the era and judging what size of glass to use in serving.

Pony	=	1	Ounce
Liqueur Glass	=	1	Ounce
Wine Glass	=	2	Ounces
Bar Glass	=	3	Ounces
Gill	=	4	Ounces
Champagne Glass	=	4½	Ounces
Mixing Glass	=	12	Ounces
Soda Water Glass	=	12	Ounces

The following ingredients are those most often called for in making drinks of the Civil War era. The **Glossary** contains definitions of most of the ingredients.

Brandies

Applejack
Brandy (Grape)
Cherry
Cognac
Orange
Peach Brandy

Brewed Beverages

Ale
Bitter Ale
Old (Aged) Ale
Scottish Ale

Porter

London Porter

Dublin (Irish) Stout
Guinness Stout

Gins

Domestic
Dutch
English

Liqueurs

Chartreuse
Cinnamon Water (Cinnamon Liqueur) (Creme de Canelle)
Curacao (Cointreau)
Kirschwasser
Maraschino
Cream de Noyeau
Vanilla Cordial

Rums

Batavia (Dutch) Arrack
Jamaica
St. Croix (Santa Cruz)

Whiskeys

Bourbon
Irish
Islay (Scotch Whiskey)
Rye
Scotch

Wines

Catawba

Champagne
Claret (Red Wine)
Hockheimer (Hock) (Rhine)
Madeira
Moselle
Moselle, Sparkling
Port
Sauterne
Sherry
Sherry, Pale
White Wine

Page from a 19th century supply trade catalog showing an Absinthe drip glass, Julep straws, and working bottles.

Bitters

Angostura
Orange

Essences & Tinctures

Aromatic Tincture
Essence of Cinammon
Essence of Cloves
Essence of Ginger
Essence of Peppermint
Oil of Cinnamon
Pineapple Oil
Tincture of Capsicum

Fruits & Juices

Apples
Apple Cider
Cherries
Lemon Juice
Lemons
Lime Juice
Limes
Orange Juice
Oranges
Peaches
Pineapples
Raspberries
Red Currents (Raisins)
Strawberries

Spices

Allspice
Balm (fresh sprigs)
Borage (fresh sprigs)
Cayenne Pepper
Cinnamon
Cloves

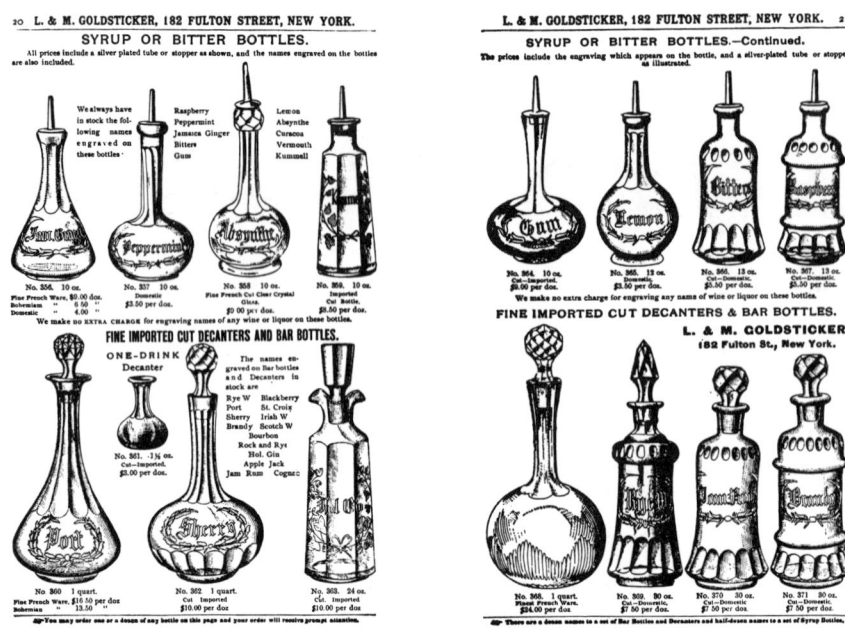

Page from a 19th century supply trade catalog showing bar bottles and decanters.

Coriander Seeds
Ginger
Mace
Mint (fresh sprigs)
Nutmeg
Vanilla (Liquid & Stick)
Verbena (fresh sprigs)

Sugar

Black Stripe Molasses
Brown Sugar
Capillaire
Fine Sugar
Granular Sugar
Honey
Loaf Sugar
Powdered Sugar
Rock Candy

Syrups

Ginger Syrup
Gum (Arabic) Syrup
Lemon Syrup
Orgeat Syrup
Pineapple Syrup
Raspberry Syrup
Simple Syrup
Strawberry Syrup

Waters

Orange Flower Water
Seltzer
Soda

Page from a 19th century supply trade catalog showing flasks, demijohns, and bottles.

Page from a 19th century supply trade catalog showing liquor labels sold in lots of 100 to 1000. Purveyors of imitation liquors frequently purchased bogus labels to make inferior goods appear "respectable."

Miscellaneous

Aerated (Sparkling) Lemonade
Ale Yeast
Almonds (Sweet & Bitter)
Biscuits
Calf's Foot Jelly (Unflavored Gelatin)
Coconut Milk
Cream of Tartar
Cucumbers
Eggs
Ginger Beer
Green Tea
Guava Jelly
Milk
Toast
Vinegar

Ale and Beer Drinks

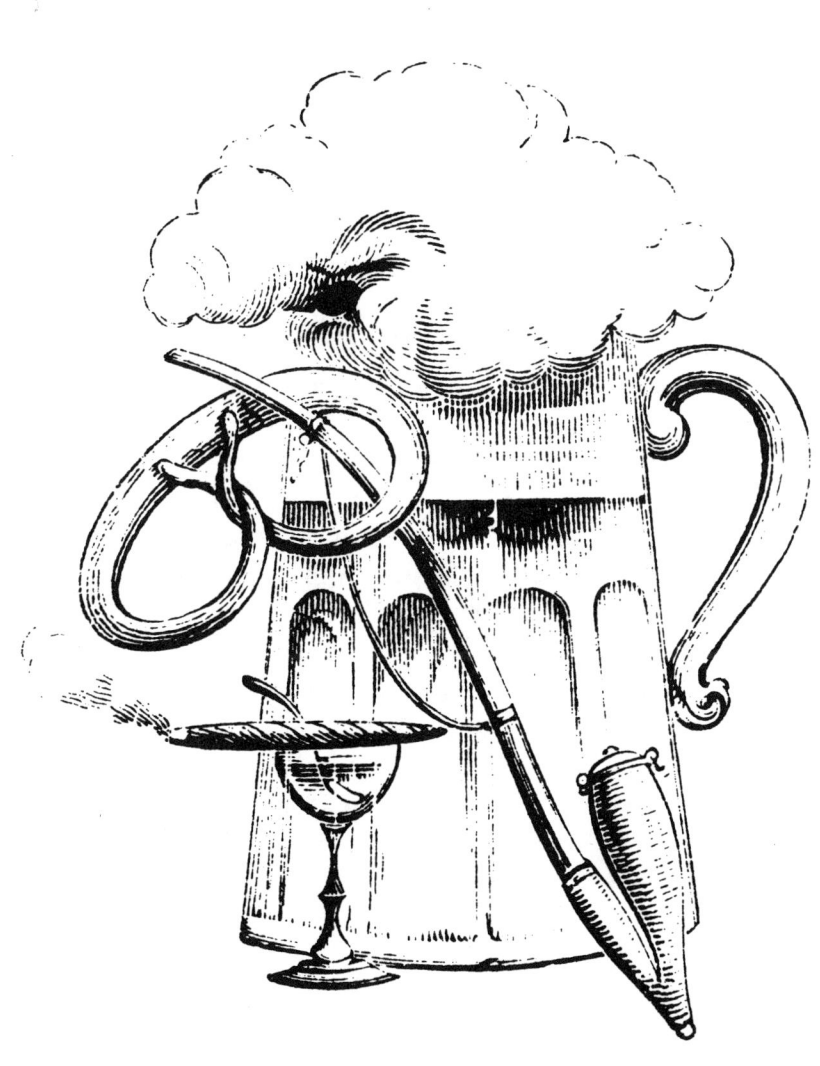

Over the past decade there has been a resurgence of small American "micro-breweries" producing specialty ales, beers and porters. Companies like Anchor Steam are making brews that have not been commonly available since Prohibition. Thanks to the production of these breweries, and the continued success of venerable British firms like Guinness, it is possible to enjoy an authentic *'Arf and 'Arf* or *Shandy Gaff*—drinks that were famous among the immigrant soldiers of a century ago.

About Ales, Beers, and Porters

The terms ale and beer were often used interchangeably during the 1860s. There was little difference between many ales and beers due to primitive equipment, poor ingredients and unskilled brewmasters. Soldiers in the field were not particular, although civilians frequently deplored the inferior beverages sold as beer and ale.

Ales, beers, porters, and stout of the 1860s were usually served at room temperature, or heated if they were used in mixed drinks. As early as 1805 New Englanders were harvesting lake ice, storing it in subterranean ice houses, and shipping it abroad, packed in the holds of ships. A thriving trade in ice existed by the 1840s, but it was too expensive for common use and storage was a problem. Mechanical ammonia and ether ice-making machines were invented before the war, but were novelties until the 1870s. In the South, only lucky drinkers who had access to expensive lake ice shipped from the North were fortunate enough to have their summer beer cold.

Ale

Ale is more aromatic and fuller-bodied than beer. It is made from water and malt (or malt and cereal grains). Ale is fermented at higher temperatures than beer, which causes the yeast to rise to the top of the brew, making ale a top-fermented brew.

Ale, porter, and stout "traveled" better than lager beer (see below). Scotch, Irish, and English ales were bottled and shipped to the U.S. and the Confederacy in an unrefrigerated, unpasteurized state. They were available either bottled or in the keg.

Bitter ale had bitter hops added for distinctive flavoring. It was usually more heavily bodied than plain ale. Old ale was aged various lengths of time for smoothness and character. Scotch ale was imported from Scotland and, like the Scots, was regarded to be strong and hardy. Stout is dark, malty ale with a distinctive taste gained by adding roasted barley to the brew.

Beer

American beers of the 1860s were lagered (cellered) beers, the type usually consumed today. True lager beers of the 1860s were like modern lager beers—clear, light and effervescent. They were brewed from a mixture of malt, hops and water called wort. Corn, grits and cracked rice were sometimes added to the wort to impart flavoring and character.

The process of brewing was simple but exacting. After the wort was properly mixed, it was allowed to ferment and then lagered (stored) for aging and sedimentation. Beer ferments at lower temperatures than ale to allow the yeast to fall to the bottom of the brew, making it a bottom-fermented brew.

Carbonation was added after lagering. Beer was commonly carbonated by the injection of "carbonic acid gas." Carbonic acid gas was made in an apparatus that exposed marble chips to a stream of sulfuric acid. The resulting energetic gas was collected and piped into the beer. Inferior beers were carbonated by adding carbonate of soda and cream of tartar, which created gas in the beer—and the consumer. Like ale, beers of the 1860s were usually served warm for want of refrigeration.

Unlike ale, beer did not travel well unless refrigerated. The first "practical" refrigerated cars, cooled by filling their double walls with huge quantities of ice, were introduced at the Centennial Exposition in 1876. Civil War beer was unpasteurized—Louis Pasteur did not develop the heat pasteurization process until 1860, and most postwar brewmasters considered it detrimental to the taste of beer.

Messers. Wesley Boulds, John Reinhardt, and Frank Blandford at Paducah, Kentucky. (Dean S. Thomas)

Porter

Porter is a heavy, bittersweet, and dark member of the beer and ale family made from charred malt, which gives it a dark brown appearance. Stout is porter with a higher alcohol content.

Ginger Beer

Ginger Beer was a sparkling drink and mixer made in Britain and Ireland. It was made of fermented ginger, sugar, yeast, cream of tartar and water. Ginger beer was available in both alcoholic and alcohol free versions; it is now commonly made as a nonalcoholic soft drink. A recipe for making ginger beer is provided (#15).

The ales, beers and porters served in posh hotels and saloons were usually genuine and of quality. They were often used as ingredients in punches and mixed drinks. William Terrington, author of *Cooling Cups and Dainty Drinks*, (1869) advised that:

Ale and beer (mixed drinks) cups should be made with good sound ale, and drunk from the tankard; being more palatable and presentable in this way than in glasses.

Soldiers in the field drank ale, beer, or porter of uncertain quality, and any way they could get it. What they drank was often crudely made of impure ingredients by untrained brewmasters or a complete sham (See the chapter "A Humbug and A Nuisance As Regards Health" for such recipes.)

1
Ale Cup

Cinnamon
Cloves
Allspice
Nutmeg
1 Gill of Sherry
Ale
Ginger Beer

Macerate [soak] ¼ ounce of cinnamon, 2 cloves, 1 allspice, and a little grated nutmeg in a gill of sherry. Allow to steep for two hours, then strain, press, and place in a jug. Pour in 2 pints of ale [Burton No. 1 ale was recommended] and 4 bottles of ginger beer [Rawlings brand of alcoholic ginger beer was recommended]. This is a drink that will make you forget all care; a little ice is an improvement in the glass.

Cooling Cups and Dainty Drinks, 1869

2
Ale Cup or Jehu's Nectar

Ginger
1 Wine Glass Gin and Bitters
1 Pint Good Ale

Into a quart pot grate some ginger; add a wine glass of gin-

and-bitters; then a pint of good ale (heated). This should be drunk while it is frothing.

Cooling Cups and Dainty Drinks, 1869

3
Hot Ale Cup

1 Quart Ale
2 Wine Glasses Gin
1 Wine Glass Sherry
2 Tablespoons Bitters
Cloves
Cinnamon
4 Tablespoons Sugar

Heat the ale, add the rest of the ingredients, and stir.

Cups and their Customs, 1863

4
Ale Cup

1 Bottle Edinburgh [Scottish] Ale
2 Bottles Ginger Beer
½ Gill Ginger Syrup
1 Slice of Cucumber
1 Pint Shaved Ice

Mix the above together, stir well, and pour into thin glasses.

Cooling Cups and Dainty Drinks, 1869

5
Ale Flip

1 Quart Ale
2 Egg Whites
4 Egg Yolks
4 Tablespoons Moist Sugar
Grated Nutmeg

Put the ale in a saucepan over a fire and let it boil; have ready the whites of two eggs and the yolks of four, well beaten up separately; add them by degrees to four tablespoons moist sugar, and half a nutmeg grated. When all are well mixed, pour on the boiling ale by degrees, beating up the mixture continuously; then pour it rapidly backward and forward from one jug to another, keeping one jug raised high above the other, until the flip is smooth and finely frothed. This a good remedy to take at the commencement of a cold.

Bon-Vivant's Companion, 1862

6
Ale Punch

1 Quart Mild Ale
1 Glass White Wine
1 Glass Brandy
1 Glass Capillaire
Juice of 1 Lemon
1 Thin Lemon Peel

Combine the above in a punch bowl, grate nutmeg on top, and add a bit of toasted bread.

Bon-Vivant's Companion, 1862

7
Ale Sangaree

Ale
1 Teaspoon Sugar
Nutmeg

Dissolve one teaspoon of sugar in a tablespoon of water. Fill a tumbler with ale, add the sugar water and grate nutmeg on top.

Bon-Vivant's Companion, 1862

8
'Arf and 'Arf
[Half and Half]
(Use a Large Bar Glass)

In London this drink is made by mixing half porter and half ale, in America it is made by mixing half new and half old ale.

Bon-Vivant's Companion, 1862

9
Beer Cup

1 Bottle Guinness Stout
2 Bottles of Ginger Beer
1 Wine Glass Gin
1 Wine Glass Cloves
1 Liqueur Glass Syrup of Ginger
French Roll (Bread) toasted a nice brown, not burned.

Combine the above in a small punch bowl and add powdered sugar to taste. Just before serving, sprinkle a small quantity of grated nutmeg on top. Serve in a silver cup.

Gentleman's Table Guide, 1873

10
Cooper

1 Pint Dublin [Irish] Stout
1 Pint London Porter

Mix in a goblet and serve.

Cooling Cups and Dainty Drinks, 1869

11
Copus Cup

2 Quarts Ale
4 Wine Glasses Brandy
3 Wine Glasses Noyeau
1-½ Pounds Sugar
Juice of 1 Lemon

Heat the ale and add the above ingredients. Toast a slice of bread, stick a slice of lemon on it and decorate with a dozen cloves. Float the bread on the liquid, over which grate some nutmeg, and serve hot.

Cups and their Customs, 1863

12
Early Birds
or
Purl

1 Quart Ale
1 Tablespoon Powdered Ginger and Nutmeg
1 Gill Cold Ale
1 Glass Spirits
2 Ounces Moist Sugar
3 Fresh Eggs

Heat the ale and mix in the spices. Add the cold ale, eggs and sugar and whisk up. When well frothed up, add the warm ale, by degrees, and a glass of spirits. When this is done drink immediately.

Cooling Cups and Dainty Drinks, 1869

13
Egg Flip

3 Eggs
3 Ounces Sugar
1-½ Pints Strong Ale
2 Wine Glasses Gin or Rum

Add the whites and yolks of three eggs beaten together, with three ounces of sugar, to half a pint of strong ale. Heat the mixture nearly to the boiling point, then put in the gin or rum (the former being preferable), with some grated nutmeg and ginger. Add another pint of hot ale, and pour the mixture frequently from one jug to another before serving.

Cups and their Customs, 1863

14
Freemason's Cup

1 Pint Scotch Ale
1 Pint Mild Beer
½ Pint Brandy
½ Pound Sugar
Grated Nutmeg

This cup may be drank either hot or cold.

Cups and their Customs, 1863

15
Ginger Beer

1-¼ Ounce Cream of Tartar
1-½ Ounce Bruised Ginger
2 Pounds Loaf Sugar
2 Lemons

½ Pound Sugar
2 Tablespoons Good Ale Yeast

Combine the cream of tartar and ginger, add lemon peel, and bruise this mixture in a mortar with one-half pound of sugar. Put it, the loaf sugar, and the lemon juice in a pan. Add 6 quarts of boiling water and add two tablespoonfuls of good ale yeast when the boiling water has cooled to lukewarm. Let this ferment for ten hours, drain clear, cork tight and tie down. The mixture will be fit for use in ten hours.

Cooling Cups and Dainty Drinks, 1869

16
John Bright

1 Pint Stout
1 Pint Bitter Ale

Mix in a goblet and serve.

Cooling Cups and Dainty Drinks, 1869

A group of Civil War sutlers in the field with liquor and tobacco. (U.S. Army Military History Institute)

17
Mother-in-Law

Mix half old and half bitter ale in a goblet.

Cooling Cups and Dainty Drinks, 1869

18
Porteree or Porter Sangaree

Porter
1 Teaspoon Sugar
Nutmeg

Dissolve 1 teaspoonful of sugar in a tablespoonful of water.
Fill a tumbler with porter, add the sugar water and grate
nutmeg on top.

Bon-Vivant's Companion, 1862

19
Rumfustian

This is the singular name bestowed upon a drink very much
in vogue with English sportsmen, after their return from a day's
shooting, and is concocted thus:

1 Pint Gin
1 Bottle Sherry
1 Quart Strong Beer
Nutmeg
Lemon Peel
Sugar

The yolks of a dozen eggs are well whisked up, and put into
a quart of strong beer; to this is added a pint of gin; a bottle
of sherry is put into a saucepan, with a stick of cinnamon, a
nutmeg grated, a dozen large lumps of sugar, and the rind of
a lemon peeled very thin; when the wine boils, it is poured
upon the gin and beer, and the whole is drunk hot.

Bon-Vivant's Companion, 1862

20
Shandy Gaff

1 Pint Good Ale
1 Bottle Ginger Beer

Mix in a goblet and serve.

Cooling Cups and Dainty Drinks, 1869

The earliest reference to the drink Shandygaff *(sic)* is an 1853 citation from The Oxford Universal Dictionary.

21
Wait a Bit

1 Pint Scotch Ale
1 Bottle Aerated Lemonade

Place in a goblet, mix, add one pint of lump ice and serve.

Cooling Cups and Dainty Drinks, 1869

A. Foulke's sutler store in winter camp at Brandy Station, Virginia, February 1863. (U.S. Army Military History Institute)

Cobblers

Champagne Cobbler.

Like the julep, this delicious potation is an American invention, although it is now a favorite in all warm climates. The "cobbler" does not require much skill in compounding, but to make it acceptable to the eye, as well as to the palate, it is necessary to display some taste in ornamenting the glass after the beverage is made. [Provided is an] illustration showing how a cobbler should look when made to suit an epicure.

Bon-Vivant's Companion, 1862

The Cobbler, Jerry Thomas wrote, is an American invention known as far back as 1809. It was originally a northern summer drink "requiring small skill in its composition," essentially a mint-less julep using wine instead of higher-proof brandy or gin. Only Northerners and a few Southerners who had access to lake ice stored in ice houses could obtain the shaved ice necessary for many cobbler recipes.

22
Catawba Cobbler
(Use a Large Bar Glass)

2 Wine Glasses Catawba Wine
1 Teaspoon Sugar

Dissolve one teaspoon of sugar in one tablespoon of water. Fill a tumbler with shaved ice, the dissolved sugar, and the above ingredients. Ornament with orange slices and berries in season. Serve with straws.

Bon-Vivant's Companion, 1862

23
Champagne Cobbler
(For Four)

1 Bottle Champagne
1 Piece Lemon Peel
1 Piece Orange Peel
1 Tablespoon Sugar

Mix the above in a large bar glass. Fill each of four tumblers one-third full of shaved ice, and fill the balance with wine. Ornament in a tasty manner with berries in season. This beverage should be sipped through a straw.

Bon-Vivant's Companion, 1862

24
Claret Cobbler
(Use a Large Bar Glass)

2 Wine Glasses Claret Wine
1 Teaspoon of Sugar

Dissolve one teaspoon of sugar in one tablespoon of water. Fill a tumbler with shaved ice, the dissolved sugar and the above ingredients, and ornament with sliced orange and berries in season. Serve with straws.

Bon-Vivant's Companion, 1862

25
Hock or Rhine Wine Cobbler
(Use a Large Bar Glass)

2 Wine Glasses Hock Wine
1 Teaspoon Sugar

Dissolve one teaspoon of sugar in one tablespoon of water. Fill a tumbler with shaved ice, the dissolved sugar and the above ingredients and ornament with sliced orange and berries in season. Serve with straws.

Bon-Vivant's Companion, 1862

26
Sauterne Cobbler
(Use a Large Bar Glass)

2 Wine Glasses Sauterne Wine
1 Teaspoon Sugar

Dissolve one teaspoon of sugar in one tablespoon of water.
Fill a tumbler with shaved ice, the dissolved sugar and the
wine and ornament with sliced orange and berries in season.
Serve with straws.

Bon-Vivant's Companion, 1862

27
Sherry Cobbler
No. 1

2 Wine Glasses Sherry
1 Tablespoon Brandy
2 Teaspoons Powdered Sugar
2 or 3 Small Pieces Lemon

Fill a tumbler three-fourths full of pounded ice and add the
above ingredients. Pour the mixture rapidly from this
tumbler to another several times, throw in half a dozen
strawberries, and then drink the mixture through a straw or
a stick of macaroni.

Cups and Their Customs, 1863

28
Sherry Cobbler
No. 2
(Use a Large Bar Glass)

2 Wine Glasses Sherry
2 or 3 Slices Orange
1 Tablespoon Sugar

Fill a tumbler with shaved ice, shake well, add the above, and
ornament with berries in season.

Bon-Vivant's Companion, 1862

29
Sherry Cobbler
No. 3

½ Pint Sherry
½ Gill Curacao
Juice of ½ Orange
Peel of 1 Orange
1 Tablespoon Sugar

Fill a large bar glass with a pint of pounded ice; add the sherry, Curacao and orange juice; top with one tablespoon of sugar and the peel of an orange.

Cooling Cups and Dainty Drinks, 1869

30
Sherry Cobbler
No. 4

¼ Pint Sherry
1 Ounce Sugar
3 Slices Orange or
A Few Strawberries or Raspberries

Fill up a tumbler with planed [shaved] ice, add the above, mix well, and top with a little powdered sugar or nutmeg on top. Serve with straws.

Cooling Cups and Dainty Drinks, 1869

31
Whiskey Cobbler
(Use a Large Bar Glass)

2 Wine Glasses Whiskey
1 Tablespoon Sugar
2 or 3 Slices Orange

Fill a tumbler with ice, add the above ingredients and shake well. Imbibe through a straw.

Bon-Vivant's Companion, 1862

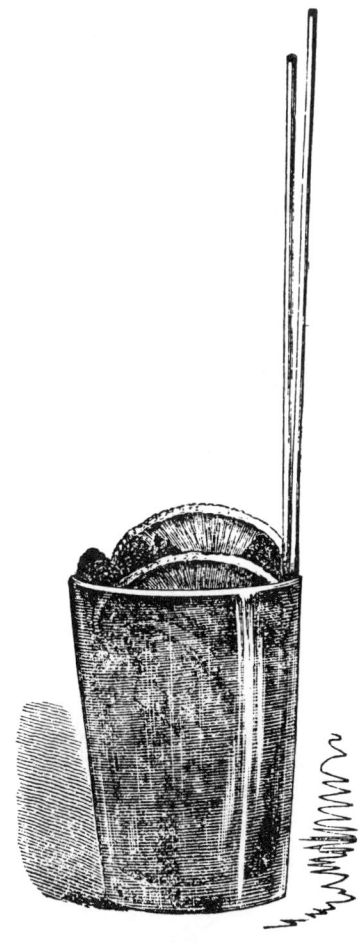

Whiskey Cobbler.

Cocktails

Champagne Cocktail.

> The "Cocktail" is a modern invention, and is generally used on fishing and other sporting parties, although some patients insist that it is good in the morning as a tonic.
>
> *–Jerry Thomas*

Jerry Thomas considered cocktails to be "modern" inventions because they did not descend from 17th and 18th century European drinks. We would consider them venerable as the word cocktail has been used to signify a category of drinks since at least 1806.

Elaborate tales have been told, and countless theories advanced, about the origin of the word cocktail. The source of the name was lost long ago. The authors favor the argument that cocktail is a corruption of one of two French terms: *coquetier*, a type of egg-cup sometimes used as a drinking glass; or *coquetel*, a wine cup used in Bordeaux.

In the 1860s, cocktails were primarily tavern-bottled combinations of wine, bitters and fruit juice. The custom of making before dinner cocktails at home was not widespread until after 1900. Instead, tavern-keepers prepared "bottles of cocktail" for special customers to keep on their sideboards and to take on hunting and fishing trips, picnics and jaunts to the races. Recipe #32 is similar to these early cocktails, except that brandy, whiskey or gin is recommended over wine. Brandy and Cognac ultimately replaced wine in cocktails.

Interestingly, since many cocktail recipes contained fruit juice, plus the extracts of roots, bark and herbs, they were regarded as healthful. The chronically ill and believers in preventive medicine were urged to consume them as early morning tonics "to fortify the inner man."

In comparison to the dry drinks of today, cocktails of a century ago were sweet drinks containing sugar and syrups. The first truly dry Martinis did not appear until the 1890s. Most aficionados of modern dry cocktails may dislike the old recipes. Persons who like soft drinks and sweets will find them pleasant.

32
Bottled Brandy Cocktail

⅔ **Quart Brandy**
1 Pony Glass Bitters
⅓ **Quart Water**
½ **Pony Curacao**
1 Wine Glass Gum Syrup

To make a splendid bottle of brandy cocktail use the above ingredients.

The author has always used this recipe in compounding the above beverage for connoisseurs. Whiskey and gin cocktails, in bottles, may be made by using the above recipe, and substituting those liquors instead of brandy.

Bon-Vivant's Companion, 1862

33
Brandy Cocktail

¼ **Pint Brandy**
2 Fluid Drams Essence of Ginger
Sugar

Place the above in a tumbler, fill up with hot water, and sweeten to taste.

Cooling Cups and Dainty Drinks, 1869

34
Brandy or Gin Cocktail

¼ **Pint Brandy or Gin**
½ **Gill Curacao**
1 Tablespoon Bitters
½ **Gill Ginger Syrup**

**1 Pint Ice
Lemon Juice**

Place the above in a tumbler that has had the rim moistened
with lemon juice. Mix with a spoon and serve.

Cooling Cups and Dainty Drinks, 1869

35
Champagne Cocktail
(For Six)

**1 Bottle Cold Champagne
1 or 2 Dashes Bitters
1 Piece Lemon Peel
$\frac{1}{2}$ Teaspoon Sugar**

Fill tumbler one-third full of broken ice, add the above ingredients, and fill with champagne. Shake well and serve.

Bon-Vivant's Companion, 1862

36
Cider Cocktail

**1 Pint Good Cider
1 Slice Lemon
$\frac{1}{2}$ Pint Shaved Ice or Iced Soda Water
1 Drop Tincture Columba
1 Tablespoon Curacao**

Add the above to a large tumbler, mix with a spoon, and
serve.

Cooling Cups and Dainty Drinks, 1869

"Columba" (actually Calumba) is the root of a plant native to
Mozambique, Jateorhiza palmata. It was used as a mild tonic and
stomachic. The formula for tincture of Columba is unknown; a drop
of good bitters or stomach bitters would be a reasonable substitute in
this case.

37
Gin Cocktail
(Use a Claret Glass)

1 Wine Glass Gin
2 or 3 Dashes Angostura Bitters
2 Dashes Curacao
3 or 4 Dashes Gum Syrup
1 Lemon
1 Teaspoon Powdered Loaf Sugar

Fill the tumbler one-third full of shaved or rasped ice and all
the above ingredients. Shake all well together and strain.
Epicures rub the rim of the glass round with lemon, and dip
into powdered sugar or candy. It gives a frosted appearance.

Gentleman's Table Guide, 1873

38
Japanese Cocktail
(Use a Small Bar Glass)

1 Tablespoon Orgeat Syrup
½ Teaspoonful Bogart's Bitters
1 Wine Glass Brandy
1 or 2 Pieces Lemon Peel

Fill the tumbler one-third with ice, and stir well with a spoon.

Bon-Vivant's Companion, 1862

39
Whiskey Cocktail
No. 1
(Use a Small Bar Glass)

1 Wine Glass Whiskey
2 Dashes Bogart's Bitters
3 or 4 Dashes Gum Syrup

1 Piece Lemon Peel

Fill a small bar glass one-third full of fine ice, add the above, shake and strain into a fancy wine glass.

Bon-Vivant's Companion, 1862

40
Whiskey Cocktail
No. 2

1 Lemon Peel
2 Fluid Drams Tincture of Columba
2 Drops Tincture of Capsicum
½ Gill of Whiskey

Infuse these in a tumbler, strain, and add 1 pint of ice. If preferred, drink warm.

Cooling Cups and Dainty Drinks, 1869

41
Whiskey Cocktail
No. 3

½ Gill Whiskey
1 Teaspoon Bitters
2 Drops Essence of Cinnamon

Add the above to a large tumbler, sweeten with syrup, add ½ pound of pounded ice, mix with a spoon, and serve.

Cooling Cups and Dainty Drinks, 1869

Crustas

Brandy Crusta.

> The "Crusta" is an improvement on the cocktail and is said to have been invented by Santina, a celebrated Spanish caterer.
>
> *–Jerry Thomas*

Little is known about the Crusta other than the fact that it was a popular southern drink before the War. Jerry Thomas attributed the drink to Santina, the owner of a popular Spanish cafe-saloon in the French Quarter of New Orleans.

Part of the crusta was showmanship. The rim of a red wine glass was coated with sugar in much the same way as the rim of a modern Margarita glass is coated with salt. Then a lemon was pared in the same manner as an apple to yield a long, continuous peel. The lemon peel was carefully and aesthetically arranged in the glass. Finally, the liquor was added, completing the drink.

42
Brandy Crusta
(Use a Small Bar glass)

1 Wine glass Brandy
2 Dashes Curacao
1 Dash Boker's Bitters
3 or 4 Dashes Gum Syrup
1 Dash Lemon Juice

Before mixing the above ingredients, prepare a red wine glass as follows:

Rub a sliced lemon around the rim of the glass, and dip it in pulverized white sugar, so that the sugar will adhere to the edge of the glass. Pare half a lemon the same as you would an apple (all in one piece) so that the paring will fit in the wine-glass, as shown in the cut.

Put the above ingredients into a small whiskey glass filled one-third full of shaved ice, shake up well and strain the liquid into the red wine glass prepared as directed above. Then smile.

Bon-Vivant's Companion, 1862

43
Gin Crusta

Gin crusta is made like the brandy crusta using gin instead of brandy.

Bon-Vivant's Companion, 1862

44
Whiskey Crusta

The whiskey crusta is made like the brandy crusta using whiskey instead of brandy.

Bon-Vivant's Companion, 1862

Liquor is very evident at this gathering in Dr. David McKay's quarters with the Army of the James. (U.S. Army Military History Institute)

Fancy Drinks

There were two-fisted drinkers in every social class.

Thousands of mixed "fancy drinks" were invented between 1840 and 1900; every serious bartender claimed to have devised at least one new drink. Most of their recipes have been lost because they were never written down. Some were novelty drinks like the flaming *Blue Blazer, White Tiger's Milk* and the speeding *Locomotive*. Others honored famous personages including General Grant, Stonewall Jackson and President Lincoln.

Few of these mixological fantasies remained popular for more than a decade. Tastes changed, novelty wore off and customers sought new thrills. But in these drinks we can glimpse a little of the humor, ingenuity and personalities of the men who created them.

45
Asses' Milk

½ Gill Rum
1 Bottle Aerated Lemonade

Combine the above ingredients in a mixing glass, two-thirds full of fine ice. Stir, and strain into a large bar glass.

Cooling Cups and Dainty Drinks, 1869

Asses' "Milk" is the polite name for this beverage. Combining golden rum and yellow lemonade may yield a beverage similar in color to a donkey byproduct—but not milk!

46
Badminton
(Use a Silver Cup)

1 Bottle Claret
½ Peeled, Middle-sized Cucumber
Four Ounces Powdered Sugar
A Little Nutmeg

Peel half of a middle-sized cucumber, and put it into a silver cup, with four ounces of powdered sugar, a little nutmeg, and a bottle of claret. When the sugar is thoroughly dissolved, pour in a bottle of soda water, and it is fit for use.

Bon-Vivant's Companion, 1862

Badminton was named, not after the racquet game, but after a famous English hunt, promoted by the Duke of Beaufort, that was named for his residence in Gloucestershire, Badminton Hall. His son, Henry Charles Fitzroy Somerset, invented the better known game of Badminton in 1868.

47
Black Stripe

1 Wine Glass Rum
1 Drop Pineapple Oil
½ Ounce Molasses

This drink can either be made in summer or winter. If the former season, add the above and mix in one tablespoon of water and cool with shaved ice. If in the latter, add the above and fill up the tumbler with boiling water. Add a little grated nutmeg on top. [Editors' Note: Several recipes omit the pineapple oil, which may be difficult to locate.]

Cooling Cups and Dainty Drinks, 1869
Bon-Vivant's Companion, 1887 Edition

Named for the famous Black Stripe Molasses.

48
Blue Blazer
(Use Two Large Silver-plated Mugs, with Handles)

1 Wine Glass Scotch Whiskey
1 Wine Glass Boiling Water

Put the whiskey and the boiling water in one mug, ignite the liquid with fire, and while blazing mix both ingredients by pouring them four or five times from one mug to the other, as represented in the cut. If well done this will have the appearance of a continued stream of liquid fire.

Sweeten with one teaspoon of pulverized white sugar, and serve in a small bar tumbler, with a piece of lemon peel.

Jerry Thomas, famous author of **How to Mix Drinks** *or* **Bon-Vivant's Companion** *(1862), mixing his famous Blue Blazer.*

The "blue blazer" does not have a very euphonious or classic name, but it tastes better to the palate than it sounds to the ear. A beholder gazing for the first time upon an experienced artist, compounding this beverage, would naturally come to the conclusion that it was a nectar for Pluto rather than Bacchus. The novice in mixing this beverage should be careful not to scald himself. To become proficient in throwing the liquid from one mug to the other, it will be necessary to practice for some time with cold water.

Bon-Vivant's Companion, 1862

Jerry Thomas invented this famous drink in San Francisco between 1849 and 1851. It was a great favorite among miners of the California Gold Rush. Although rarely attributed to Thomas, the recipe can still be found in bartending manuals 140 years later. Use care if you attempt to make it!

49
Brandy and Gum
(Use a Small Bar Glass)

Brandy
Gum Syrup

Put a piece of ice in a tumbler, add a dash of gum syrup, and hand it to your customer with a bottle of brandy.

Bon-Vivant's Companion, 1862

See the section on *Gum Syrup* in the **Glossary.**

50
Burnt Brandy and Peach
(Use a Small Bar Glass)

1 Wine Glass Cognac
2 or 3 Slices Dried Peaches
½ Tablespoon White Sugar

Put one wine glass of Cognac and one-half tablespoon of white sugar in a small saucer and ignite it. Place the dried fruit in a glass and pour the Cognac over it. This drink is very popular in the Southern States, where it is sometimes used as a cure for diarrhoea.

Bon-Vivant's Companion, 1862

51
Brandy Champerelle

1 Wine Glass Brandy
1 Wine Glass Curaao
1 Wine Glass Bitters

Mix the above with ice.

Cooling Cups and Dainty Drinks, 1869

52
Brandy Scaffa
(Use a Wine Glass)

1 Pony Brandy
1 Pony Maraschino
2 Dashes Angostura Bitters

Bon-Vivant's Companion, 1862

Scaffa is believed to be a corruption of the French *chafau* or *shaffaut*, meaning something supportive such as a scaffolding. In other words, this drink is a good "bracer."

53
Ching Ching

1 Gill Old Rum
1 Drop Essence of Peppermint
2 Drops Essence of Cloves on a Piece of Sugar
1 Slice Orange

Mix the above and pour into a soda water glass filled with fine ice.

Cooling Cups and Dainty Drinks, 1869

The name is a corruption of an Anglo-Chinese salutation or greeting *Ts'ing-Ts'ing*.

54
Columbia Skin
(also called **Scotch Whiskey Skin**)
(Use a Small Bar Glass)

1 Wine Glass Scotch Whiskey
1 Piece of Lemon

Place the above in a small bar glass and fill it one-half full of boiling water. This is a Boston drink.

Bon-Vivant's Companion, 1862

Skins were drinks made with boiling water and high proof alcohol. Drink one of these too fast and it will take the skin off your throat.

55
Corpse Reviver
(Use a Wine Glass)

½ **Wine Glass Brandy**
½ **Glass Maraschino Liqueur**
2 Dashes Boker's Bitters

Place the above in a wine glass and serve.

Gentleman's Table Guide, 1873

56
General Grant
(For 2)
(Use a Large Mixing Glass)

1 Pint Bottle Champagne
1 Wine Glass Cognac
1 Gill Pineapple Syrup
1 Gill Strawberry Syrup
1 Sliced Orange

Add the above to a large mixing glass along with a tumbler of shaved ice, shake well and strain.

Gentleman's Table Guide, 1873

Named, of course, for General Ulysses S. Grant (1822-1885). Many drinks were named after Union and Confederate officers during and after the war.

57
Gin and Pine
(Use a Wine Glass)

1 Bottle Gin
Heart of a Pine Log

Split a piece of the heart of a green pine log into fine splints, about the size of a cedar lead-pencil, take two ounces of the same and put into a quart decanter, and fill the decanter with gin.

Let the pine soak for two hours, and the gin will be ready to serve.

Bon-Vivant's Companion, 1862

This drink tastes much like pine cleaner and may not be all that healthy.

58
Gin and Tansy
(Use a Wine Glass)

1 Bottle Gin
Tansy

Fill a quart decanter one-third full of tansy, and pour in gin to fill up the balance. Serve to customer in a wine glass.

Bon-Vivant's Companion, 1862

Tansy (Tanacetum Vulgare) is also called Cow Bitters and Button Bitters. It is a weedy, fragrantly bitter plant native to Europe but naturalized in the eastern U.S. and Canada. Tansy is said to be slightly poisonous, so avoid mixing this drink. Victorians probably liked it because of their fondness of bitters, and in Gin and Bitters.

59
Hot Spiced Rum
(Use a Small Bar Glass)

1 Wine Glass Jamaica Rum
1 Teaspoon Sugar
1 Teaspoon Mixed Allspice and Cloves
1 Piece Butter as Large as $\frac{1}{2}$ a Chestnut

Place the above in a tumbler, fill with hot water, stir well, and serve.

Bon-Vivant's Companion, 1862

60
Hour Before (The Battle)

1 Wine Glass Sherry or Madeira
1 Dash Boker's or Angostura Bitters

Add the above to a mixing glass, stir, and serve in a wine glass.

Cooling Cups and Dainty Drinks, 1869

This drink gets its name from the officers' habit of taking a stiff drink, often with bitters, before a battle.

61
Knickerbocker
(Use a Small Bar Glass)

1 Wine Glass Santa Cruz Rum
Teaspoon Curacao
2 Teaspoons Raspberry Syrup
Lime or Lemon

Take one-half a lime, or lemon, squeeze out the juice, and put rind and juice in the glass. Add the raspberry syrup, Santa Cruz rum, and Curacao; mix well. Cool with shaved ice; shake up well, and ornament with berries in season. If this is not sweet enough, put in a little more raspberry syrup.

Bon-Vivant's Companion, 1862

Knickerbockers were the original Dutch settlers of New York. The word became a synonym for New Yorkers.

62
Knickerbocker a' La Madame

Pint Sherry or Madeira
Pint Lemon Water
1 Small Bottle Seltzer Water

Combine the above in a large glass with one-quarter pint of shaven ice.

Cooling Cups and Dainty Drinks, 1869

63
Knickerbocker a' La Monsieur

1 Wine Glass Jamaica Rum
1 Tablespoon Curacao
Juice of 1 Lemon or Orange
2 Tablespoons Raspberry Syrup

Add the above to a soda water glass, mix and add shaved ice.

Cooling Cups and Dainty Drinks, 1869

64
Lamb's Wool

1 Quart Old Ale
Ginger
Nutmeg
Eight Apples
Sugar

Roast eight apples; mash them, and add one quart of old ale; press and strain; add grated ginger and nutmeg; sweeten to taste with sugar; warm, and drink while warm.

Cooling Cups and Dainty Drinks, 1869

This drink, when properly made, was said to have been as smooth as lamb's wool.

65
Locomotive

1 Pint Burgundy Wine
1 Liqueur Glass Curacao
Yolks of 2 Eggs
1 Ounce Honey
Essence of Cloves

Put two yolks of eggs into a goblet with an ounce of honey, a little essence of cloves, and a liqueur glass of Curacao. Add a pint of high Burgundy made hot, whisk well together, and serve hot in glasses.

Bon-Vivant's Companion, 1862

A delightful drink reminiscent of a slightly thick, sweet sangria heavy on the orange juice.

66
Nectar for 90° in the Shade

½ Gill Whisky
1 Bottle Iced Soda Water
Lemon Ice

Put a lemon ice in a soda water glass, add one half gill of whisky and a bottle of iced soda water, mix and serve.

Cooling Cups and Dainty Drinks, 1869

67
Nightcap
(Use a Pint Tankard)

Pint Sound Old Ale
1 Wine Glass Wine, Gin or Brandy
A Few Drops Essence of Cloves
Sugar

Mix the above, sweeten to taste, and make hot, but do not boil.

Gentleman's Table Guide, 1873

68
Peach and Honey
(Use a Small Bar Glass)

1 Wine Glass Peach Brandy
1 Tablespoon Honey

Mix the above and stir with a spoon.

Bon-Vivant's Companion, 1862

A popular southern drink.

69
President Lincoln
(Use a Soda Water Glass)

1 Liqueur Glass Kirschwasser
1 Shilling's Worth of Cherry Ice
A Bottle Soda

Combine the above in a large soda water glass and serve.

Gentleman's Table Guide, 1873

Named, of course, after the Union commander-in-chief. One of many drinks that bore his name during the war and after his assassination.

Washington as Commander in Chief, carte-de-visite photo by E. & H.T. Anthony. Back reads: "The original of this picture is in possession of General Lee, at Richmond. It was captured by our forces, and returned to its owner by the Government. This copy was made while it was in Washington."

70
President Washington
(Use a Soda Water Glass)

1 Wine Glass Brandy
1 Tablespoon Honey
1 Glass Strawberry Syrup
or
10 Fresh Strawberries
Juice of a Lemon

Add the above ingredients to a soda water glass, and fill up with shaved ice. If the fruit is used, it must be brushed with the honey, crushed and strained. Serve with two straws.

Gentleman's Table Guide, 1873

George Washington was as a hero of both North and South during the war.

71
The Prima Donna

1 Wine Glass Sherry
Yolk of 1 Egg
A Very Little Cayenne Pepper

Beat the yolk of one egg in a glass of sherry; add a very little cayenne pepper, and serve.

Cooling Cups and Dainty Drinks, 1869

This potent and spicy drink was said to sing like a prima donna, the principal female singer in an opera.

72
Ribs

1 Gill Cognac
1 Tablespoon Gum Arabic Syrup
1 Gill Shaved Ice

Place the above in a large tumbler, mix and serve.

Cooling Cups and Dainty Drinks, 1869

The combination of Cognac and a Gum Arabic sugar syrup would surely stick to your ribs. See the **Glossary** for a *Gum Syrup* recipe.

73
Sherry and Egg
(Use a Small Bar Glass)

1 Wine Glass Sherry
1 Egg

Pour in about one wine glass of sherry. Then break in the glass one fresh egg.

Bon-Vivant's Companion, 1862

74
Sleeper

1 Gill Old Rum
Juice of $\frac{1}{2}$ Lemon
2 Eggs Yolks
6 Cloves
6 Coriander Seeds
Cinnamon
1 Ounce Sugar

Two a gill of old rum add an ounce of sugar, two yolks of eggs, and the juice of half a lemon; boil half a pint of water with six cloves, six coriander seeds, and a bit of cinnamon; whisk all together and strain them into a tumbler.

Bon-Vivant's Companion, 1862

This warm drink is an excellent relaxer.

75
Spider

1 Gill Gin
1 Bottle Lemonade

Add to a large bar glass filled with lump ice, stir well, and serve.

Cooling Cups and Dainty Drinks, 1869

76
Stone Fence
(Use a Large Bar Glass)

1 Wine Glass Bourbon Whiskey
Sweet Cider

Add the whiskey and two or three lumps of ice to a large bar glass; fill up the glass with sweet cider, and serve.

Bon-Vivant's Companion, 1862

A smooth southern drink.

77
Stone Wall
(Also called a **Brandy and Soda**)
(Use a Large Bar Glass)

1 Wine Glass Cognac Brandy
Soda Water

Place one wine glass of Cognac in a large bar glass, add half
a glass of fine ice and fill up with plain soda.

Bon-Vivant's Companion, 1862

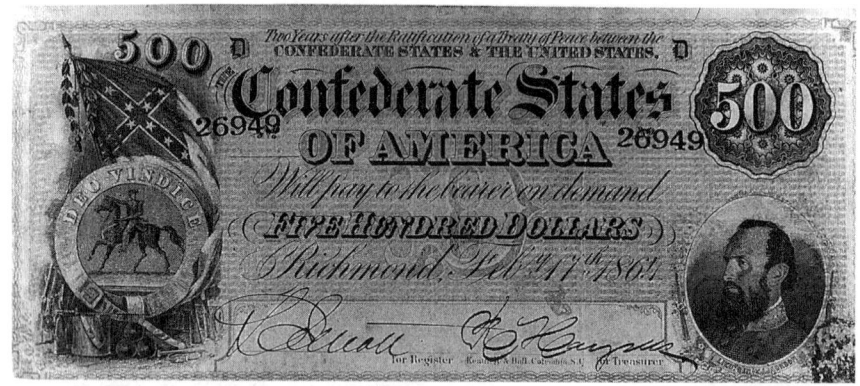

78
Stonewall Jackson
(Use a Soda Water Glass)

1 Wine Glass Brandy
Apple Cider

Fill a soda water glass one-third full of shaved ice, add one

wine glass of brandy, fill up with cider, insert two straws, and
serve.

Gentleman's Table Guide, 1873

Named after Confederate General Thomas Jonathan "Stonewall"
Jackson (1824-1863). This drink is basically a variation of a stone fence.

79
Bottled Velvet

1 Bottle Moselle Wine
½ Pint Sherry
Lemon Peel
Sugar
Sprig of Verbena

To a large bowl, add a half bottle of Moselle, half a pint of
sherry, the peel of a lemon, not too much, so as to have the
flavor predominate. Then add two tablespoons of sugar, a
sprig of verbena. Mix well, strain and ice.

Bon-Vivant's Companion, 1862

This mixture of wine, sherry and lemon herb has a very smooth
taste, hence the appellation "velvet." Verbena (Lippia Citriodora) is a
subshrub native to Chile and Peru. Its leaves have a strong lemon
scent, and they are used in beverages and perfume.

80
Whiskey Skin
(Use a Small Bar Glass)

1 Wine Glass Scotch or Irish Whiskey
1 Piece of Lemon Peel

Add the above to a tumbler and fill one-half full of boiling
water. This is called a Columbia Skin in Boston.

Bon-Vivant's Companion, 1862

See comments under Columbia Skin (#54).

81
White Lion
(Use a Small Bar Glass)

1 Wine Glass Santa Cruz Rum
$\frac{1}{2}$ Teaspoon Curacao
$\frac{1}{2}$ Teaspoon Raspberry Syrup
$\frac{1}{2}$ a Lime
1-$\frac{1}{2}$ Teaspoons Powdered Sugar

Place the above in a small bar glass, mix well, ornament with berries in season, and cool with shaved ice.

Bon-Vivant's Companion, 1862

82
White Tiger's Milk
(Use a Large Bowl)
(For Two)

$\frac{1}{2}$ Gill Applejack
$\frac{1}{2}$ Gill Peach Brandy
1 Quart Pure Milk
$\frac{1}{2}$ Teaspoon Aromatic Tincture
White of an Egg

Pour in the mixed liquor into the milk, stirring all the while, then sprinkle with nutmeg.

Bon-Vivant's Companion, 1862

See the **Glossary** for the recipe for *Aromatic Tincture*.

83
Yard of Flannel

1 Quart Ale
6 Eggs
Four Tablespoons Brown Sugar
A Little Nutmeg

Put a quart of ale in a tinned saucepan on the fire to boil; in the meantime, beat up the yokes of four eggs, with the whites of two eggs, adding four tablespoons of brown sugar and a little nutmeg; pour on the ale by degrees, beating up, so as to prevent the mixture from curdling; then pour back and forward repeatedly from vessel to vessel, raising the hand to as great a height as possible—which process produces the smoothness and frothing essential to the good quality of the drink.

Bon-Vivant's Companion, 1862

This is excellent for a cold, and, from its fleecy appearance, is designated "a yard of flannel." It is also known as an Egg Flip.

–Jerry Thomas

Number two of a series of five carte-de-visite photos probably taken by H. Skinner of Fulton, New York, in 1862. Drinking was an important release for soldiers during the Civil War. (William Welling)

Fixes

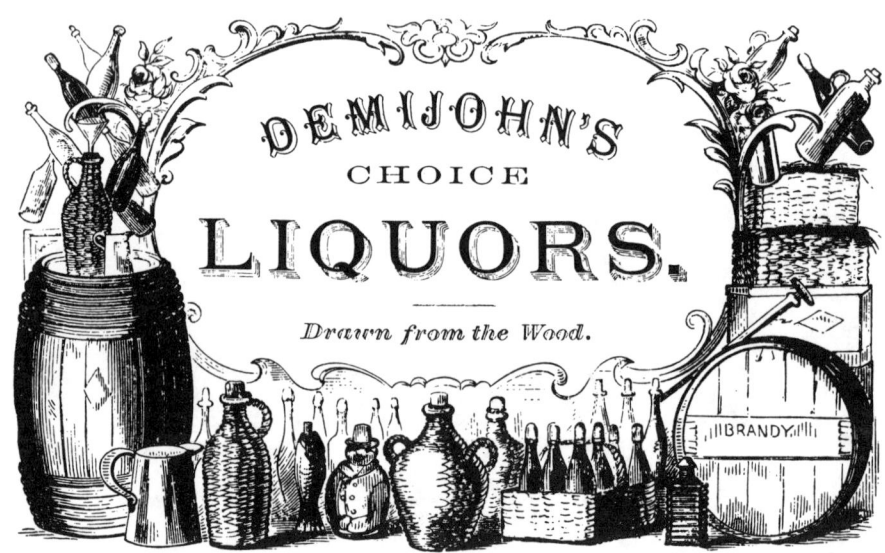

Little is known about the origin of Fixes, among the simplest and most popular 19th century iced drinks. They were apparently unknown in the 18th century, but by 1862 two versions, the *Brandy Fix* and the *Gin Fix*, are listed in *The Bon-Vivant's Companion*.

A basic Fix is made of applejack, gin, brandy or rum mixed with fruit syrups, lemon juice and sugar poured over ice. For the convenience of the customer, a fix was normally served with both a straw and a fruit spoon.

84
Brandy Fix
(Use a Small Bar Glass)

1 Wine Glass Brandy
½ Wine Glass Water
¼ Lemon
1 Tablespoon Sugar

Fill a tumbler two-thirds full of shaved ice and add the above. Stir with a spoon, and dress the top with fruit in season.

Bon-Vivant's Companion, 1862

85
Gin Fix
(Use a Small Bar Glass)

1 Wine Glass Gin
½ Wine Glass Water
¼ Lemon
1 Tablespoon Sugar

Fill a tumbler two-thirds full of shaved ice and add the above. Stir with a spoon, and dress the top with fruit in season.

Bon-Vivant's Companion, 1862

86
Santa Cruz Rum Fix
(Use a Small Bar Glass)

1 Wine Glass Santa Cruz Rum
$\frac{1}{2}$ Wine Glass Water
$\frac{1}{4}$ Lemon
1 Tablespoon Sugar

Fill a tumbler two-thirds full of shaved ice and add the above. Stir with a spoon, and dress the top with fruit in season.

Bon-Vivant's Companion, 1862

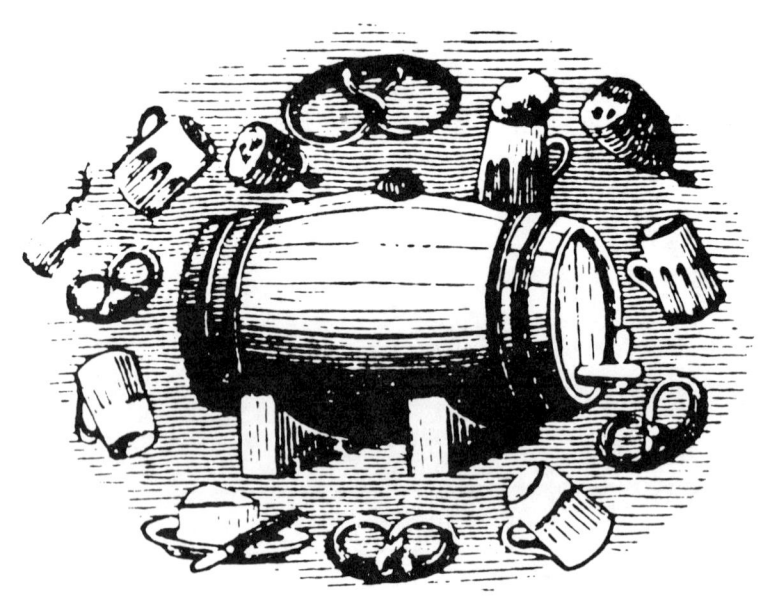

Flips

Scene at the Saratoga Races.

Folklore attributes the invention of the Flip to the rural British. It was a hot beverage, made with ale, wine, rum or whatever liquor was handy, mixed with sugar, eggs and spices. One noted beverage authority, Edward R. Emerson, described how a Flip was finished off using a tool known as a flip dog.

> No one in the olden days could make flip in a manner to please those who really knew what the drink was, unless they had a well-seasoned flip dog. A flip dog is not much on the bark, for it is only a bar of iron shaped somewhat like a poker, and when it was in use had to be heated red-hot and then plunged into the glass containing the flip, which by the way was made, according to the taste of the drinker, either from ale, cider, or wine, and highly spiced; sometimes an egg was stirred in to give it a little more body.

Sailors considered flips to be their favorite beverage, although they seldom had all the necessary ingredients, especially fresh eggs, to make it at sea.

American bartenders never used flip dogs to make the drink and they modified the basic recipe beyond recognition. About the only steady ingredient was the egg, although several so-called flips (see: Cold Brandy Flip #87) omitted the egg as well. What had once been a simple hot drink was made in many versions both hot and cold.

Ale Flip
See Ale and Beer Drinks

87
Cold Brandy Flip
(Use a Tumbler)

1 Wine Glass Brandy
1 Teaspoon Powdered Sugar or Rock Candy
1 Toasted Biscuit
1 Egg Yolk

Place one teaspoon of powdered sugar or rock candy and one wine glass of brandy in a tumbler. Fill the tumbler one-third full of boiling water, mix well, and place a small cracknell or biscuit (toasted) on top. Grate a small quantity of nutmeg on top. The yolk of one new laid egg is an improvement.

Gentleman's Table Guide, 1873

88
Hot Brandy Flip
(Use a Tumbler)

1 Wine Glass Brandy
1 Teaspoon Sugar

Fill the tumbler one-third full of hot water, mix in the above ingredients, and place a toasted cracker on top, and grate nutmeg over it.

Bon-Vivant's Companion, 1862

89
Egg Flip
No. 1

2 Wine Glasses Cognac
1 Wine Glass Old Jamaica Rum
4 New Laid Eggs
1/2 Dozen Large Lumps of Sugar

Beat up, in a jug, four new laid eggs, omitting two of the whites; add half a dozen large lumps of sugar, and rub these well in the eggs, pour in boiling water, about half a pint at a time, and when the jug is nearly full, throw in two tumblers of Cognac brandy, and one of old Jamaica rum.

Bon-Vivant's Companion, 1862

90
Egg Flip
No. 2

1 Quart Ale
4 Egg Yolks
2 Egg Whites
4 Tablespoons Brown Sugar
Nutmeg

Put a quart of ale in tin saucepan on the fire to boil. In the meantime, beat up the yolks of four, with the whites of two eggs, adding two tablespoons of brown sugar and a little nutmeg. Pour on the ale by degrees, beating up, so as to prevent the mixture from curdling. Then pour back and forth repeatedly from vessel to vessel, raising the hand to as great a height as possible—which process produces the smoothness and frothing essential to the good quality of the flip. This is excellent for a cold, and, from its fleecy appearance, is sometimes designated "a yard of flannel."

Bon-Vivant's Companion, 1862

91
Egg Flip
No. 3

1 Quart Good Ale
1 Wine Glass Gin or Whisky
6 Egg Yolks
1-½ Pounds Moist Sugar

Place one quart of good ale into a clean saucepan over a fire. Put the yolks of six fresh eggs in a basin and add half a grated nutmeg and one-half pound of moist sugar. Beat the mixture adding one wine glass of gin or whisky. As the ale simmers, skim the froth off into a basin containing the eggs, sugar, nutmeg and liquor. When the ale nearly boils (do not let it boil) pour it into the mixture, stirring all the while. If you use the whites of eggs as well, only use three eggs.

Cooling Cups and Dainty Drinks, 1869

92
Excellent Egg Flip

1 Gill Good French Brandy
2 Egg Yolks
1 Gill Boiling Cinnamon Water
2 Drops Oil of Cinnamon

Boil the cinnamon water. Beat up, in a basin, the yolks of two new laid eggs. Pour in the boiling cinnamon water, a small portion at a time. When the basin is nearly full, add one gill of good French brandy and two drops oil of cinnamon. This agreeable stimulant and restorative is of great service when used in cases of extreme exhaustion.

Cooling Cups and Dainty Drinks, 1869

93
Rum Flip

1 Gill Old Rum or Brandy
1 Quart Ale
4 Eggs
4 Ounces Moist Sugar
1 Teaspoon Grated Nutmeg or Ginger

Keep grated ginger and nutmeg with a little fine dried lemon peel, rub together in a mortar.

To make a quart of flip: Put the ale on the fire to warm, and beat up three or four eggs with four ounces of moist sugar, a teaspoon of grated nutmeg or ginger, and a gill of good old rum or brandy. When the ale is near to boil, put it into one pitcher, and the rum and eggs, & etc., into another. Turn it from one pitcher to another 'til it is as smooth as cream.

Bon-Vivant's Companion, 1862

Juleps and Smash

Fancy Brandy Smash.

No other mixed drink is as well known as the *Mint Julep*. The Oxford English Dictionary traces the word "julep" back many centuries to the Persian *gul-ab* or Arabic *julab*, indicating rosewater or a cooling drink containing opium. Whatever its original composition, the beverage was brought to Europe during medieval times and reached England by 1400. Over the next few centuries the English continued to distort the Middle Eastern name of the drink, calling it *Julap, Juloup, Jewlip*, and *Juleb*. Whatever they called it, it was made from a spiced sugar and wine and liquor.

British colonists brought julep to the American Colonies in the 17th century when southern savants took control and made the *Mint Julep* an institution. The basic ingredients of the *Mint Julep* were fixed between 1760 and 1770, although some sources contend that the it was invented in 1858 at the Old White Springs in Virginia's Allegheny Mountains. Author and retired British naval captain Frederick Marryatt contradicted this in 1836 by writing "the mint julep [is], with the thermometer at 100 degrees, one of the most delightful and insinuating potations that ever was invented . . ."

Surprisingly, the julep was not commonly made with bourbon until well after the Civil War. Instead, the liquors of choice were brandy (preferably the finest available Cognac), Madeira or claret. Persons fond of bourbon juleps should sample one made with Cognac before scoffing.

Despite its Middle Eastern and British origins, the julep soon became steeped in southern tradition. In 1887, Jerry Thomas reprinted a newspaper article that appeared in a Georgia newspaper describing the aura surrounding the true *Mint Julep:*

Probably the old-fashioned julep is in its decadence as a public drink, but it does not follow that the art of constructing this famous Southern refresher is lost. On the contrary, we have knowledge of several old-fashioned gardens where the mint bed under the southern wall still blooms luxuriantly; where white fingers of household angels still come every day about this time of the year and pluck a few sprays of the aromatic herb to build a julep for poor old shaky grandpa, who sits in the shady corner of the veranda with his feet on the rail and his head busy with the olden days. In such a household the art is still preserved. With her sleeves rolled up, the rosy granddaughter stirs sugar in a couple of tablespoonfuls of sparkling water, packs crushed ice to the top of the heavy cut glass goblet, pours in the mellow whiskey until an overflow threatens and then daintily thrusts the mint sprays into the crevices. And the old man, rousing from his dreams, blesses the vision which seems to rise up from the buried days of his youth, and with his gay nose nestling peacefully in the nosegay at the summit of his midday refresher, quaffs the icy drink, and with a long-drawn sigh of relief sinks back to dream again until the dinner bells sounds its hospitable summons. The mint julep still lives, but it is by no means fashionable. Somehow the idea has gotten abroad that the mint ought to be crushed and shaken up with water and whiskey in equal proportions. No man can fall in love with such a mixture. Poor juleps have ruined the reputation of the South's most famous drink.

To please their southern customers, mixologists put together several versions of the *Mint Julep*, as well as juleps featuring champagne, gin, rum and whiskey. Everyone had their favorite recipe, and many rounds were downed to determine which was the best. The authors are particularly fond of *The Real Georgia Mint Julep* developed in the 1850s or 1860s but first recorded in the 1880s.

The proper way to drink a julep is to slowly drink the mixture through a straw (or a piece of hollow pasta) as the ice melts into the liquor. This permits the ice to carry along the essence of the mint. The mixing of the ice water, mint essence and liquor is what makes the drink special.

We have combined juleps with Smash because of the similarity of the drinks. Jerry Thomas wrote that a smash was "simply a julep on a small plan." Since the first known reference to a Smash dates from 1859, and there is little difference between the two drinks, it is possible that "Smash" was originally American slang for "Julep."

94
Brandy Julep
(Use a Large Bar Glass)

1-$\frac{1}{2}$ Wine Glasses Cognac Brandy
2-$\frac{1}{2}$ Tablespoons Water

1 Tablespoon White Sugar
3 or 4 Sprigs of Fresh Mint

Dissolve one tablespoon of white pulverized sugar in two
and one-half tablespoonfuls of water. Take two sprigs of
fresh mint and press them well in the sugar and water, until
the flavor of the mint is extracted; add one wine glass of
Cognac brandy, and fill the glass with fine shaved ice, then
draw out the sprigs of mint and insert them in the ice with
the stems downward, so that the leaves will be above, in the
shape of a bouquet. Serve with a straw.

Bon-Vivant's Companion, 1862

95
Gin Julep
No. 1

The Gin Julep is made the same as the Brandy Julep (No. 1),
substituting gin for the brandy.

Bon-Vivant's Companion, 1862

96
Gin Julep
No. 2

1 Gill Gin
½ Gill Maraschino
4 Sprigs Mint

Place the above ingredients in a large bar glass, stir, and fill
the glass with 1 pint of pounded ice. Serve with straws.

Cooling Cups and Dainty Drinks, 1869

97
Mint Julep
No. 1

1-½ Wine Glasses Cognac Brandy
1 Dash Jamaica Rum
2-½ Tablespoons Water
1 Tablespoonful White Sugar
3 or 4 Sprigs Fresh Mint

Dissolve one tablespoon of white pulverized sugar in two and one-half tablespoons of water. Take two sprigs of fresh mint and press them well in the sugar and water, until the flavor of the mint is extracted; add one wine glass of Cognac brandy, and fill the glass with fine shaved ice, then draw out the sprigs of mint and insert them in the ice with the stems downward, so that the leaves will be above, in the shape of a bouquet; arrange berries, and small pieces of sliced orange on top in a tasty manner, dash with Jamaica rum, and sprinkle white sugar on top. Place as straw as represented in the cut, and you will have a julep that is fit for an emperor.

Bon-Vivant's Companion, 1862

A Civil War era Mint Julep. Note the abundant use of mint.

98
Mint Julep
No. 2

1 Wine Glass Brandy
Juice of 1 Orange
3 Sprigs Fresh Mint
1 Tablespoon Rum
1 Tablespoon Crushed Rock Candy

Take three sprigs of fresh gathered mint; put them into a
soda water glass; add two tablespoons of sugar, one wine
glass of brandy, the juice of one orange; in ten minutes fill
the glass up with shaven ice; draw the mint out, and rear-
range them, stem upwards; lay the thin peel of an orange on
top; pour on one tablespoonful of rum and one tablespoon
of crushed white rock candy; suck through straws—let me
add—devoutly.

Cooling Cups and Dainty Drinks, 1869

99
Pineapple Julep
(For a party of Five)

1 Gill Old Gin
1 Bottle Sparkling Moselle Wine
1 Gill Raspberry Syrup
1 Pineapple
Juice of 2 Oranges

Peel, slice and cut up a ripe pineapple into a glass bowl; add
the juice of two oranges, a gill of raspberry syrup, a gill of
maraschino, a gill of old gin, a bottle of sparkling Moselle,
and about a pound of pure ice in shaves [sic]; mix, ornament
with berries in season, and serve in flat glasses.

Bon-Vivant's Companion, 1862

On the subject of **Pineapple Julep**, William Terrington (*Cooling Cups and Dainty Drinks,* 1869) wrote:

Epicures rub the lips of the tumbler with a piece of fresh pineapple, and the tumbler itself is often incrusted [sic] outside with stalactites of ice. As the ice melts, you drink.

100
The Real Georgia Mint Julep

¾ **Wine Glass Cognac Brandy**
¾ **Wine Glass Peach Brandy**
12 Sprigs Tender Mint Shoots

Put the mint in the tumbler, add the sugar, having previously dissolved it in a little water, then the brandy, and lastly, fill up the glass with shaved ice. Stir with a spoon but do not crush the mint. This is the genuine method of concocting a Southern mint julep, but whiskey may be substituted for brandy if preferred.

Bon-Vivant's Companion, 1887 Edition

101
Rum Julep

Substitute rum for brandy in Mint Julep No. 1.

Gentleman's Table Guide, 1873

102
Season Ticket Julep

2 Glasses Dry Sherry
1 Bottle of Cider
1 Gill Good Lemonade
1 Teaspoon Orange Flower Water
3 Sprigs Mint

Place the above in an ice pitcher, sweeten to taste, and add 1 pound of shaven ice.

Cooling Cups and Dainty Drinks, 1869

103
Whiskey Julep

Substitute whiskey for brandy in Mint Julep No. 1, but omit all fruits and berries.

Bon-Vivant's Companion, 1862

104
Smash

1 Wine Glass Brandy, Gin, Rum or Whiskey
1 Tablespoon Water
1 Tablespoon White Sugar

Take two sprigs of fresh mint and press them well in the sugar and water, until the flavor of the mint is extracted; add one wine glass of Cognac brandy, and fill the glass two-thirds full of shaved ice, then draw out the sprigs of mint and insert them in the ice with the stems downward, so that the leaves will be above, in the shape of a bouquet. Lay two small pieces of orange on top, and ornament with berries in season.

Bon-Vivant's Companion, 1862

Lemonade and Orangeade

The toast was a part of social gatherings.

Lemonade is now thought of as a refreshing, alcohol free summer cooler. In the 1860s there were both alcohol-free and spirituous lemonades containing rum, wine or brandy.

105
American Lemonade
(Alcohol Free)

1 Tablespoon Powdered Sugar
1 Orange Slice
1 Tablespoon Raspberry Syrup
Juice of 1-$\frac{1}{2}$ Lemons

Add the juice of half a lemon, 1 tablespoon of sugar, an orange slice, and 1 tablespoon of raspberry syrup to a large soda water glass and mix well. Then, fill the glass half full of shaved ice, add the juice of a fresh lemon and stir. Ornament with berries in season and serve with two straws.

Gentleman's Table Guide, 1873

106
Italian Lemonade
(Contains Spirits)

1 Quart Sherry
2 Dozen Lemons
1 Quart Boiling Milk
2 Pounds Loaf Sugar

Pare and press two dozen lemons, pour the juice on the peels and let it remain on them all night. In the morning, add two pounds of loaf sugar, a quart of sherry, and three quarts of boiling water. Mix well, add a quart of boiling milk, and strain through a jelly bag until clear.

Bon-Vivant's Companion, 1862

107
Lemonade
No. 1
(Alcohol Free)

3 Sliced Lemons
½ Pound White or Brown Sugar
1 Gallon Water

Cut in very thin slices three lemons, put them in a basin and add half a pound of sugar. Bruise all together, add a gallon of water, and stir well. It is then ready.

Bon-Vivant's Companion, 1862

108
Lemonade
No. 2
(Contains Spirits)

Port Wine
Juice of ½ Lemon
1-½ Tablespoons Sugar
2 or 3 Orange Pieces
1 Tablespoon Raspberry or Strawberry Syrup

Place the above ingredients in a large bar glass, stir well, fill the tumbler half full of shaved ice, and the balance with water. Dash with port wine and ornament with fruits in season.

Bon-Vivant's Companion, 1862

109
Lemonade
No. 3
(Fine for Parties)
(Contains Spirits)

Sherry
Rind of Two Lemons
Juice of 3 Large Lemons
½ Pound Loaf Sugar
1 Quart Boiling Water

Rub some of the sugar, in lumps, on two of the lemons until they have imbibed all the oil from them, and put it with the remainder of the sugar into a jug; add the lemon juice (but no pips) and pour over the whole a quart of boiling water. When the sugar is dissolved, strain the lemonade through a piece of muslin, and, when cool, it will be ready for use.

The lemonade will be much improved by having the white of an egg beaten up with it; a little sherry mixed with it also makes the beverage much nicer.

Bon-Vivant's Companion, 1862

110
Orangeade

This agreeable beverage is made the same way as Lemonade No.3, substituting oranges for lemons.

Bon-Vivant's Companion, 1862

111
Orgeat Lemonade
(Alcohol Free)

½ Wine Glass Orgeat Syrup
Juice of ½ Lemon

Add the above ingredients to a large bar glass, stir well, fill the tumbler one-third full of ice and the balance with water. Shake well, and ornament with berries in season.

Bon-Vivant's Companion, 1862

Pousse Cafes

Cognac.
Chartreuse (yellow).
Curacoa (red).
Vanilla (green).
Maraschino.
Parfait d'Amour,
or Raspberry Syrup.

Cognac.
Vanilla (green).
Yolk of Egg.
Maraschino.

Pousse Cafe.   *Pousse L'Amour.*

Preparing a southern *Pousse Cafe* (French for "After Coffee") was the ultimate test of a bartender's skills. French in origin, they were layered, specialty drinks intended for show rather than serious consumption. Bartenders in old New Orleans first popularized Pousse Cafes in the 1840s and 1850s. Between 1885 and 1905 they took on the proportions of a fad in better saloons throughout the country.

Creating a pousse cafe required a "steady hand and careful manipulation." From three to twelve different cordials, syrups and brandies were poured over the back of a spoon into a cordial glass. The spoon broke the fall of the cordials, making it easier to layer them. By carefully adding the components, in order of their specific gravities, the cordials remained separate and the result was a colorful kaleidoscopic effect. If brandy was the last ingredient, it was occasionally set on fire as the drink was served.

The modern use of synthetic flavorings in cheaper cordials makes it difficult to guarantee results when recreating these drinks. Liqueurs containing imitation flavorings sometimes have different specific gravities than "true fruit" cordials.

112
Parisian Pousse Cafe
(Use a Small Wine Glass)

Add the following to a small wine glass:

$\frac{2}{5}$ **Curacao**
$\frac{2}{5}$ **Kirschwasser**
$\frac{1}{5}$ **Chartreuse**

> This is a celebrated Parisian drink.
>
> *Bon-Vivant's Companion, 1862*

113
Pousse l'Amour

½ Wine Glass Maraschino Liqueur
Vanilla Cordial
Cognac
1 Egg Yolk

This delightful French drink is described in the above engraving. To mix it fill a small wine-glass half full of maraschino, then put in the pure yolk of an egg, surround the yolk with vanilla cordial, and dash the top with cognac brandy.

Bon-Vivant's Companion, 1862

114
Santina's Pousse Cafe
(Use a Small Wine Glass)

⅓ Wine Glass Brandy (Cognac)
⅓ Wine Glass Maraschino Liqueur
⅓ Wine Glass Curacao

This delicious drink is from a recipe by Santina, proprietor of Santina's Saloon, a celebrated Spanish Cafe in New Orleans.

Bon-Vivant's Companion, 1862

Punch Bowl Drinks

"To the General and his wife!" Making a toast on a festive occasion.

Punch bowl drinks were the most popular class of beverages during the Civil War era. In fact, alcoholic beverages in general were called drinks from "the flowing bowl." Jerry Thomas listed more than 80 in his 1862 mixing manual; hundreds more have been found in other manuals of the time.

Punches were mixed for occasions as diverse as births and deaths. They were served at parties at home, group meetings at taverns and saloons, holiday celebrations, regimental reunions and wakes for departed comrades. Soldiers in the field scavenged the countryside for whiskey, corn likker, champagne and cordials. They produced mixtures both sublime and nefarious.

But there was more to mixing a proper punch bowl drink than dumping in a couple of bottles of champagne and fruit juice. Elaborate recipes included more than a dozen ingredients from imported spirits to spices and herbs. Preparation of some began days in advance with roasting of apples, steeping of flavorings and alcohol, and gathering of fruits and berries.

A wide variety of names, usually signifying different mixing techniques, have been applied to them: punches, mulls, nectars, negus, bowls, cups, shrubs and egg noggs.

Historians of drink speculate that the word Punch is derived from the Hindu word *Paunch*, the Persian *Punj*, or the Sanskrit *Pancha*. They all mean "five," for the "original" five ingredients of lime, sugar, spice, water and fermented palm juice.

Mull is a punch made from boiled wine, sugar, spices and other ingredients.

The word *nectar* was applied to any sweet drink, usually served cold.

Negus, a beverage made of hot water, port or sherry, spices and sugar was named after British Colonel Frances Negus (d. 1732) who is said to have been the inventor.

Bowls and *cups* are alternative archaic English names for punch.

Shrub is a derivative of the Arabic *shurb*, simply meaning drink.

Nogg, or *Nog*, is derived from the English *noggin*, a large pot in which the rich, egg laden beverage was prepared.

German bartenders called cold punch bowl drinks *kaltschalen*, meaning "cold bowl."

While most punches were prepared in a punch bowl, others were bottled for home consumption or to take along on outings. A few punch-type drinks were designed to be made in single drink quantities.

The following punch recipes have been selected based upon their appearance in several bartender's guides, or their novelty. After trying many, the authors' favorite is Jerry Thomas' *Rocky Mountain Punch*.

A common ingredient in many punch bowl drinks was lemon.

Jerry Thomas stated that:

> To make punch of any sort in perfection, the ambrosial essence of the lemon must be extracted by rubbing lumps of sugar on the rind, which breaks the delicate little vessels that contain the essence, and at the same time absorbs it. This, and making the mixture sweet and strong, using tea instead of water, and thoroughly amalgamating all the compounds, so that the taste of neither the bitter, the sweet, the spirit, nor the element, shall be perceptible one over the other, is a grand secret, only to be acquired by practice.

In making hot and cold punch bowl drinks, he advised that:

> you must put in the spirits before the water: in cold punch, grog, &c., the other way.

And as to the precise mixing of ingredients, well:

> The precise portions of spirit and water, or even of the acidity and sweetness, can have no general rule, as scarcely two persons make punch alike.

115
Punch

2 Wine Glasses Sherry
1 Pint Brandy
1 Pint Old Rum

Juice and Finely Pared Rind of 2 Lemons
Juice and Finely Pared Rind of 2 Seville Oranges
1 Pint Green Tea
1 Pint Boiling Water
1 Pint Calve's Foot Jelly (Plain, Unflavored Jello)
½ Pound Powdered Sugar

Extract the oil from the rind of a large lemon by rubbing it with lumps of sugar. Add the juice of two lemons and of two Seville oranges, together with the finely pared rind. Put this into a jug, with one pint of old rum, one pint of brandy, ad half a pound of powdered sugar. Stir well together, then add one pint of green tea [liquid, not the leaves] and one quart of boiling water. Mix well, and let it be served quite hot.

This is an excellent recipe for ordinary Punch, and the addition of green tea cannot be too strongly recommended. In order to give punch a delicious softness, one pint of calve's foot jelly [plain, unflavored Jello] should be added to the above recipe. The addition of two glasses of Sherry will also be found an improvement.

Cups and Their Customs, 1863

116
Punch A' La Romaine
(For a Party of 15)

1 Bottle Wine (Red or White)
1 Bottle Rum
Juice of 10 Lemons
Juice of 2 Sweet Oranges
2 Pounds Powdered Sugar
1 Orange Rind
10 Egg Whites

Take the juice of 10 lemons and 2 sweet oranges, dissolve it in two pounds of powdered sugar, and add the thin rind of

an orange. Run this through a sieve, and stir in by degrees
the whites of 10 eggs, beaten into a froth. Put the bowl with
the mixture into an ice pail, let it freeze a little, then stir
briskly into it a bottle of wine and a bottle of rum.

Bon-Vivant's Companion, 1862

Ale Punch
See Ale and Beer Drinks

117
Apple Punch

1 Bottle Claret
Slices of Apples and Lemons
Powdered Sugar

Lay in a china bowl slices of apples and lemons alternately,
each layer being thickly strewed with powdered sugar. Pour
over the fruit, when the bowl is half filled, a bottle of claret;
cover, and let it stand six hours. Then strain it through a
muslin bag, and send it up [serve it] immediately.

Bon-Vivant's Companion, 1862

118
Archbishop

1 Bottle Claret
1 Wine Glass Cherry Brandy
1 Wine Glass Orange Brandy
1 Lemon
4 Oranges
Nutmeg
Cloves
Cinnamon
Mace
Allspice
Ginger

Make several incisions in the rinds of four good sized Seville oranges. Stick cloves in, and roast them by a clear fire to a rich dark brown, not burned.

Create a spice mixture by placing small but equal quantities of cinnamon, mace, and allspice, with a race of ginger and half a pint of water, into a delicately clean saucepan. Let it boil until it is reduced by one-half, and pour the mixture over the oranges. Strain the spice mixture into another pan, juice the oranges and add to the spice mixture, and pass the combined orange juice and spice mixture through a sieve.

Meanwhile, place a bottle of good claret in a saucepan over a clear fire until it is on the point of boiling. Add to the mixture a glass of cherry brandy [Kirschwasser], one glass of orange brandy [or Curacao], the rind of a fresh lemon rubbed off on sugar, and the juice of one lemon. Now, pour your wine into a [heat resistant] bowl very hot, add the orange juice and spice mixture, grate in some nutmeg, sweeten it to taste, and serve it up with a few cloves and the curl of a fresh lemon peel.

To make a **Bishop**, substitute lemons for the oranges and good port for claret.

To make a **Cardinal**, use the oranges but substitute hock, Champagne or Moselle for the claret.

To make a **Pope**, use the oranges but substitute Burgundy or Imperial Tokay for the claret.

Gentleman's Table Guide, 1873

119
Arrack Punch

2 Wine Glasses Rum
3 Wine Glasses Arrack
2 Lemons

6 Wine Glasses Water
Sugar to Taste

In making arrack punch, you ought to put two wine glasses of rum to three of arrack. A good deal of sugar is required; but sweetening, after all, must be left to taste. Lemons and limes are also a matter of palate, but two lemons are enough for the above quantity. Put in an equal quantity of water— i.e., not five but six glasses to allow for the lemon juice, and you have a very pretty three tumblers of punch.

Most of the arrack imported into this country is distilled from rice, and comes from Batavia [Java]. It is but little used in America, except to flavor punch; the taste of it is very agreeable in this mixture. Arrack improves very much with age. It is much used in some parts of India, where it is distilled from toddy, the juice of the coconut tree.

Bon-Vivant's Companion, 1862

120
Bannister's 1829 Milk Punch

1 Quart Old Rum
2 Quarts Best Brandy
18 Lemons
Juice of 9 Seville Oranges
Juice of 9 Lemons
3 Quarts Water
2 Quarts Milk
3 Pounds of Refined Sugar
2 Grated Nutmegs

Pare 18 lemons very thin and steep the same three days in one quart best old rum. Then add two quarts best brandy, the juice of nine Seville oranges and nine lemons, three quarts of water, three pounds of double-refined sugar, and two grated nutmegs. When the sugar is dissolved, mix thoroughly, add two quarts of scalded milk, cover, and let stand two hours. Then clear it through a tammy cloth, and bottle. When required for use, it should be iced twenty minutes before drinking.

Cooling Cups and Dainty Drinks, 1869

121
Bimbo Punch

One Quart Cognac Brandy
6 Lemons
1 Pound Loaf Sugar

Steep six lemons cut in thin slices in one quart of Cognac brandy for six hours. At the end of that time the lemon must be removed without squeezing. Dissolve one pound of loaf sugar in one quart of boiling water, and add the hot solution to the arrack. Let it stand to cool. This is a delightful liqueur, and should be used as such.

Bon-Vivant's Companion, 1862

122
Brandy Shrub
(Use a Five Quart Punch Bowl)

2 Quarts Brandy
1 Quart Sherry
2 Pounds Loaf Sugar
5 Lemons

Add two quarts of brandy to the thin rinds of two lemons and the juice of five, cover it for three days, then add a quart of sherry and two pounds of loaf-sugar. Strain it through a jelly-bag, and bottle it.

Bon-Vivant's Companion, 1862

123
Hot Brandy and Rum Punch
(For a Party of 15)

1 Quart Jamaica Rum
1 Quart Cognac Brandy
1 Pound White Loaf Sugar
4 Lemons
3 Quarts Boiling Water
1 Teaspoon Nutmeg

Rub the sugar over the lemons until it has absorbed all the yellow part of the skins, then put the sugar into a punch bowl. Pour in the boiling water, stirring well. Add the rum, brandy and nutmeg, mix again, and the punch will be ready to serve.

As we have said before, it is very important, in making good punch, that all the ingredients are thoroughly incorporated. To insure success, the process of mixing must be diligently attended to. Allow a quart of punch for four persons; but this information must be taken *cum grano salis* [with a grain of salt] for the capacities of persons for this kind of beverage are generally supposed to vary considerably.

Bon-Vivant's Companion, 1862

124
Cold Brandy Punch
(An American Sensation)

1 Gill Brandy
1 Tablespoon Raspberry Syrup
2 Tablespoons White Sugar
Juice of ½ Lemon
Juice of 1 Orange
1 Slice Pineapple

Mix raspberry syrup in a tumbler with one gill of water and add the remaining ingredients. Fill with shaved ice and serve.

Cooling Cups and Dainty Drinks, 1869

125
Cold Brandy Punch

3 Pints Cognac Brandy
1-½ Pints Old Rum
1 Gill Curacao
2 Quarts Iced Filtered Water
2 Pounds Refined Loaf Sugar or Rock Candy
Juice of 6 Fresh Lemons
3 Sliced Tangerine Oranges
1 Lemon Peel Cut Thin
2 Gills Pineapple Syrup
1 Pint Pure Spring Block Ice

Add the above ingredients to a large punch bowl and mix well.

Gentleman's Table Guide, 1873

126
Canadian Punch

2 Quarts Rye Whiskey
1 Pint Jamaica Rum
6 Sliced Lemons
1 Sliced Pineapple
4 Quarts Water

Place the above in a punch bowl, sweeten to taste, and ice.

Bon-Vivant's Companion, 1862

127
Century Club Punch

2 Parts Old Santa Cruz Rum
1 Part Old Jamaica Rum
5 Parts Water

Lemons
Sugar

In any quantity, mix two parts old Santa Cruz Rum; one part old Jamaica Rum, five parts water; lemons and sugar ad lib. This is a nice punch.

Bon-Vivant's Companion, 1862

128
Champagne Cup
No. 1

1 Bottle Champagne
1 Wine Glass Curacao or Brandy
1 Bottle Soda Water
Peel of ½ Lemon
4 Pineapple or Apricot Slices
A Little White Powdered Sugar
A Few Sprigs of Borage

Place all of the above, except the soda water, in a covered jug, well immersed in rough ice for one hour. Stir all together with a silver spoon, and when the cup has been well mixed, strain it off, free from herbs, etc. Just previous to serving, add some pieces of pure spring block ice, and the soda water. Use two bottles of soda if pure spring block ice is not used. Observe not to use too much sugar in the champagne cup.

Cooling Cups and Dainty Drinks, 1869

129
Champagne Cup
No. 2

2 Bottles Champagne
1 Bottle German Seltzer Water
1 Wine Glass Madeira or Sherry

1 Glass Curacao
½ Pint Strawberries, Raspberries or Red Currants
Peel of ½ Lemon
Small Bunch of Balm
A Little Powdered Sugar

Mix as in Champagne Cup No. 1.

Cooling Cups and Dainty Drinks, 1869

130
Champagne Punch
No. 3

1 Quart Bottle Champagne
¼ Pound Sugar
1 Sliced Orange
Juice of 1 Lemon
3 Pineapple Slices
1 Wine Glass Raspberry or Strawberry Syrup

Place the above in a large punch bowl, mix well, ornament with fruits in season, and serve in champagne goblets.

This can be made in any quantity by observing the proportions of the ingredients as given above. Four bottles of wine make a gallon, and a gallon is generally sufficient for fifteen persons in a mixed party.

Bon-Vivant's Companion, 1862

131
Cherry Shrub
(Use a Two Quart Punch Bowl)

1 Quart Pitted Cherries
1 Pound Sugar
Brandy, Irish or Monongahela Whiskey

Pick ripe acid [sour] cherries from the stem and put them in an earthen pot. Place that in an iron pot of water and boil till the juice is extracted. Strain the juice through a cloth thick enough to retain the pulp and sweeten it to your taste. When perfectly clear, bottle it, sealing the cork. By first putting a gill of brandy into each bottle, it will keep through the summer. It is delicious mixed with water. Irish or Monongahela whiskey will answer instead of the brandy, though not as good.

Bon-Vivant's Companion, 1862

132
Cider Nectar
(Use a Small Punch Bowl)

1 Quart Cider
1 Glass Sherry
1 Small Glass Brandy
1 Lemon

Place the juice of half a lemon, the peel of quarter of a lemon, sugar and nutmeg to taste, and a sprig of verbena in a small earthen pot. Flavor it to taste with extract of pineapple, strain it into a small punch bowl, and ice it all well. This is a delicious beverage, and only requires to be tasted to be appreciated.

Bon-Vivant's Companion, 1862

133
Cider Punch

½ Pint Sherry
¼ Pound Sugar
Juice of 1 Lemon
Grated Nutmeg
1 Bottle Cider

On the thin rind of half a lemon pour half a pint of sherry, add remaining above ingredients. Mix it well, and if possible place it on ice. Add, before sent in, a glass of brandy and a few pieces of cucumber rind.

Bon-Vivant's Companion, 1862

Claret Punch
See **Imperial Punch**

134
Claret and Champagne Cup, A' La Brunow
(For a Party of Twenty)

The following claret and champagne cup ought, from its excellence, to be called the nectar of the Czar, as it is so highly appreciated in Russia, where for many years it has enjoyed a high reputation amongst the aristocracy of the Muscovite empire. Proportions:

3 Bottles Claret
⅔ Pint Curacao
1 Pint Sherry
½ Pint Brandy
2 Wine Glasses Raspberry Liqueur
3 Sliced Oranges
1 Sliced Lemon
A Few Green Balm Sprigs
A Few Borage Sprigs
2 Bottles German Seltzer Water
Piece of Cucumber Rind
3 Bottles Soda Water

Stir the above together and sweeten with pounded sugar until it ferments. Let it stand one hour, strain and ice it well. It is then fit for use. Serve in small glasses.

For a Champagne Cup, use champagne instead of claret and Creme de Noyau instead of raspberry liqueur.

Bon-Vivant's Companion, 1862

135
Cold Punch

2 Pints Arrack
2 Pints Port Wine
2 Pints Water
Juice of 8 Lemons
1 Pound Loaf Sugar

Mix the above in a chilled punch bowl and add ice.

Bon-Vivant's Companion, 1862

136
Curacao Punch

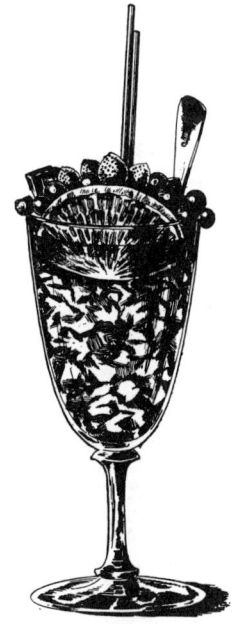

Curacoa Punch.

1 Pony Jamaica Rum
1/2 Pony Curacao
1 Pony Water
Juice of 1/2 Lemon
1 Tablespoon Sugar

Fill a tumbler with shaved ice, add the above, shake well, and ornament with fruits in season. Sip the nectar through a straw.

Bon-Vivant's Companion, 1862

137
Dry Punch

2 Gallons Brandy
1 Pint Jamaica Rum
1/2 Pint Curacao
Juice of 6 Lemons
1/2 Gallon Tea
1-1/2 Pound White Sugar

Mix the brandy, rum, Curacao and tea thoroughly. Dissolve the sugar in just enough boiling water and add to the mixture. Add more sugar and lemon juice if desired. Bottle and keep on ice for three of four days, and the punch will be ready for use, but the longer it stands the better it gets. [This punch is from an old New Orleans recipe.]

Bon-Vivant's Companion, 1862

138
Baltimore Egg Nogg
(For a Party of Fifteen)

1/2 Pint Brandy or Jamaica Rum
2 Wine Glasses Madeira
6 Pints Milk
16 Eggs
12 Tablespoons Pulverized Loaf Sugar

Take the yellow of the eggs and the sugar and beat them to the consistency of cream. Add two-thirds of a grated nutmeg, and beat well together. Then mix in the rum and Madeira. Have ready the whites of the eggs, beaten to a stiff froth, and beat them into the above described mixture. When this is all done, stir in six pints of good rich milk. There is no heat used.

Egg Nogg made in this manner is digestible, and will not cause a headache. It makes and excellent drink for debilitated persons, and a nourishing diet for consumptives.

Bon-Vivant's Companion, 1862

139
Egg Nogg
(Use a Large Bar Glass)

1 Wine Glass Cognac
½ Wine Glass Santa Cruz Rum
1 Egg
1 Tablespoon Cold Water
1 Tablespoon Fine Sugar

Dissolve the sugar in one tablespoon of cold water, and add this mixture and the remaining ingredients to a tumbler one-quarter full of shaved ice. Fill the glass with milk, shake the ingredients until they are thoroughly mixed together, and grate a little nutmeg on top. Every well ordered bar has a tin egg nogg "shaker," which is a great aid in mixing this beverage.

Egg nogg is a beverage of American origin, but it has a popularity that is cosmopolitan. At the south (sic) it is almost indispensable at Christmas time and at the north (sic) it is a favorite at all seasons.

In Scotland they call egg nogg, "auld man's milk."

Bon-Vivant's Companion, 1862

140
Hot Egg Nogg
No. 1

1 Wine Glass Cognac
½ Wine Glass Santa Cruz Rum
1 Egg
1 Tablespoon Cold Water
1 Tablespoon Fine Sugar

Dissolve the sugar in one tablespoon of cold water, and add this mixture and the remaining ingredients to a large tumbler one-quarter full of boiling water. Fill the glass with milk, shake the ingredients until they are thoroughly mixed together, and grate a little nutmeg on top. This drink is very popular in California.

Bon-Vivant's Companion, 1862

141
Hot Egg Nogg
No. 2

1 Pint Scotch Ale
1 Glass Whiskey
2 Eggs
¼ Ounce Bruised Cinnamon
¼ Ounce Grated Nutmeg
¼ Ounce Powdered Ginger
A Little Brown Sugar

Heat a pint of Scotch ale and add, while warming, the cinnamon, nutmeg and ginger. Beat up the egg yolks with a little brown sugar, pour in the ale gradually and when well amalgamated add a glass of whiskey. Stir well and serve.

Cooling Cups and Dainty Drinks, 1869

142
General Harrison's Egg Nogg

Hard Cider
1 Egg
1-½ Teaspoons Sugar
2 or 3 Small Lumps Ice

Add all of the above ingredients except the cider to a large tumbler, fill with cider, and shake well.

This is a splendid drink and is very popular on the Mississippi river. It was General Harrison's favorite beverage.

Bon-Vivant's Companion, 1862

143
Sherry Egg Nogg

2 Wine Glasses Sherry
1 Egg
1 Tablespoon White Sugar

Dissolve the sugar with a little water, break the yolk of the egg in a large glass, and put in one-quarter tumbler of broken ice. Add the dissolved sugar, fill the glass with milk, and shake up until the egg is thoroughly mixed with the other ingredients. Then, grate a little nutmeg on top and quaff the nectar cup.

Bon-Vivant's Companion, 1862

144
English Milk Punch

1 Pint Brandy
1 Pint Rum
1 Gill Arrack
1 Cup Strong Green Tea

1 Quart Boiling Water
Juice of 6 Lemons
Rinds of 2 Lemons
1 Pineapple, Peeled, Sliced and Pounded
6 Cloves
20 Coriander Seeds
1 Small Stick Cinnamon
1 Pound Sugar

Mix the above ingredients in a large jug or crock that can be sealed, adding the boiling water last. Cork this down to prevent evaporation, and allow these ingredients to steep for at least 6 hours. Then add a quart of hot milk and the juice of two lemons, mix, and filter through a jelly bag. When the punch has passed bright, put it away in tight corked bottles. This punch is intended to be iced for drinking.

Bon-Vivant's Companion, 1862

145
Gin Punch
No. 1

½ Pint Old Gin
1 Gill Maraschino
Juice of 2 Lemons
Rind of ½ Lemon
4 Ounces Gum Syrup
1 Quart Bottle German Seltzer Water

Place in a punch bowl, ice well, and serve.

Bon-Vivant's Companion, 1862

146
Gin Punch
No. 2

As a mild summer drink, and one readily made, we recommend Gin Punch.

½ **Pint Gin**
1 Glass Maraschino
2 Bottles Iced Soda Water
½ **Pint Water**
2 Tablespoons White Sugar

Mix the above, then serve.

Cups and Their Customs, 1863

147
Glasgow Punch

As to the beautiful mutual adaptation of cold rum and cold water, that is beyond all praise, being one of Nature's most exquisite achievements.

1 Part Old Jamaica Rum
5 Parts "Sherbert"
2 Limes
Juice of 2 Lemons
Lump Sugar

Melt lump-sugar in cold water, with the juice of a couple of lemons. Pass it through a fine hair strainer. This mixture is called "sherbert," and must be well mingled. Then add old Jamaica rum—one part of rum to five of sherbert. Cut a couple of limes in two, and run each section rapidly around the edge of the jug or bowl, gently squeezing in some of the delicate acid. This done, the punch is made. Imbibe.

Bon-Vivant's Companion, 1862

148
Gothic Punch
(For a Party of Ten)

4 Bottles Still Catawba Wine
1 Bottle Claret
1 Bottle Champagne
3 Sliced Oranges
1 Cut and Pieced Pineapple
10 Tablespoons Sugar

Place the Catawba wine, claret, sugar and fruit in a large
punch bowl. Let this mixture stand in a very cold place, or in
ice, for one hour or more, then add one bottle of
champagne.

Bon-Vivant's Companion, 1862

149
Iced Punch

1 Wine Glass Old Rum
1 Wine Glass Cognac
1 Wine Glass Arrack
2 Bottles Champagne
1 Pint Strong Green Tea
2 China Oranges
2 Fresh Lemons
1 Seville Orange
1 Wine Glass Pineapple Syrup
Gum Syrup
Sugar

Pare as thin as possible the rinds of two China oranges, two
fresh lemons, and one Seville orange, and infuse them for
one hour in half a pint of gum syrup. Then add to them the
juice of the fruit; make a pint of strong green tea, sweeten it
well with sugar or pulverized rock candy, and when it is
quite cold add it to the fruit and syrup, with a glass of old

rum, a glass of Cognac, one glass of arrack, one glass of pineapple syrup, and two bottles of champagne. Pass the whole through a fine sieve until it is perfectly clear. Then bottle and put it into rough ice until dinner is serve.

Gentleman's Table Guide, 1873

150
Imperial Punch

1 Bottle Claret
1 Liqueur Glass Maraschino
1 Bottle Soda Water
4 Tablespoons Powdered White Sugar
3 or 4 Slices Cucumber Rind
¼ Teaspoon Grated Nutmeg
½ Pounds Ice

Put all the ingredients into a bowl or pitcher and mix well.

Bon-Vivant's Companion, 1862

151
Imperial Raspberry Whiskey Punch
(10 Gallons)

2 Gallons Whiskey
1 Gallon Raspberry Syrup
5 Ounces Sweet Almonds
5 Ounces Bitter Almonds
1-¼ Ounce Powdered Cinnamon
⅓ Ounce Powdered Cloves
5 Ounces Plain Syrup

Boil the almonds in water, then skin. Add the cinnamon, cloves and plain syrup and macerate fine. Add to 7 gallons of water and boil for five minutes, then strain. Add 2 gallons of whiskey and one gallon of raspberry syrup.

Manufacture of Cordials, 1862

152
Hot Irish Punch

1 Wine Glass Irish Whiskey
2 Wine Glasses Boiling Water
or
1 Tablespoon Fine Sugar

This is the genuine Irish beverage. Combine one wine glass Irish whiskey with one tablespoon of fine sugar dissolved in two wine glasses of boiling water. If lemon punch, the rind is rubbed on the sugar, and a small proportion of juice is added before the whiskey is poured in.

Bon-Vivant's Companion, 1862

153
La Patria Punch
(For a Party of Twenty)

3 Bottles Iced Champagne
1 Bottle Cognac
6 Oranges
1 Pineapple

Slice the oranges and pineapple into a bowl, pour the Cognac over them and let them seep for a couple of hours, then, in with the champagne and serve immediately.

Bon-Vivant's Companion, 1862

154
Light Guard Punch
(For a Party of Twenty)

3 Bottles Champagne
1 Bottle Pale Sherry
1 Bottle Cognac
1 Bottle Sauterne

1 Sliced Pineapple
4 Sliced Lemons
Sugar

Add the above to a punch bowl, sweeten to taste, mix well, cool with a large lump of ice, and serve immediately.

Bon-Vivant's Companion, 1862

155
Milk Punch - English

Put the following ingredients into a very clean pitcher, in the following order:

Juice of 6 Lemons
Rind of 2 Lemons
1 Pound Sugar
1 Peeled, Sliced and Pounded Pineapple
6 Cloves
20 Coriander Seeds
1 Small Cinnamon Stick
1 Pint Brandy
1 Pint Rum
1 Gill Arrack
1 Cup Strong Green Tea
1 Quart Boiling Water

Cork this down to prevent evaporation, and allow these ingredients to seep for at least six hours. Then add a quart of hot milk and the juice of two lemons, mix, and filter through a jelly bag. When the punch is past bright, put it away in tightly corked bottles. This punch is intended to be iced for drinking.

Bon-Vivant's Companion, 1862

Mississippi Punch.

156
Mississippi Punch
(For a Single Serving)

1 Wine Glass Brandy
$\frac{1}{2}$ Wine Glass Jamaica Rum
$\frac{1}{2}$ Wine Glass Bourbon Whiskey
$\frac{1}{2}$ Wine Glass Water
$\frac{1}{4}$ Large Lemon
1-$\frac{1}{2}$ Tablespoons Powdered White Sugar

Place the above in a large tumbler filled with shaved ice. Shake well, and to those who like their draughts "like linked sweetness long drawn out," let them use a glass tube or a straw to sip the nectar through. The top of this punch should be ornamented with small pieces of orange, and berries in season. [For a large party, multiply the above by the number of imbibers and mix in a punch bowl.]

Bon-Vivant's Companion, 1862

157
National Guard Seventh Regiment Punch

1 Wine Glass Brandy
1 Wine Glass Catawba Wine
1 Dash Jamaica Rum
Juice of $\frac{1}{4}$ Lemon
Raspberry Syrup to Taste
1 Tablespoon Sugar

Fill a large bar glass with shaved ice, add the above, shake and mix thoroughly. Ornament with slices of orange, pineapple and berries in season, and dash with Jamaica rum. This delicious beverage should be imbibed through a straw.

Bon-Vivant's Companion, 1862

158
Nectar Punch for Bottling

4-$\frac{1}{2}$ Pints Rum
Juice and Rinds of 15 Lemons
2 Quarts Boiling Hot Milk
2 Quarts Cold Water
2-$\frac{1}{2}$ Pounds Loaf Sugar
1 Grated Nutmeg

Infuse the peel of fifteen lemons in a pint and a half of rum for forty-eight hours. Add two quarts of cold water with three additional pints of rum, the juice of the lemons, two quarts of boiling hot milk, and one grated nutmeg. Let the mixture stand twenty-four hours, covered close. Then add and mix two and a half pounds of loaf sugar. Strain this through a flannel bag till quite fine, and bottle it for use. It is fit to use as soon as bottled.

Bon-Vivant's Companion, 1862

159
None Such Punch

6 Bottles Claret
1 Bottle Brandy
1 Bottle Sherry
1 Bottle Soda Water
½ Pint Green Tea
Juice of 3 Lemons
½ Chunked Pineapple

Add the above to a large vessel and sweeten with white sugar to taste. Strain into a bottle immediately and keep one month before using.

Bon-Vivant's Companion, 1862

160
Nuremberg Punch
(For a Party of Fifteen)

1 Bottle French Red Wine
⅓ Quart Batavia Arrack
Juice of 2 Oranges
1 Small Piece Orange Peel
¾ Pound Loaf Sugar
1 Quart Boiling Water

Take three-quarters of a pound of loaf sugar, press upon it, through muslin, the juice of two or more good sized oranges. Add a little of the peel, cut very thin, pour upon the mixture a quart of boiling water, with the third part of that quantity of Batavia arrack, and a bottle of hot, but not boiling, red or white French wine—red is best. Stir together. This is excellent when cold, and will improve by age.

Bon-Vivant's Companion, 1862

A punch of German origin named after the city of Nuremberg.

161
Orange Punch

$\frac{1}{2}$ **Pint Porter**
$\frac{3}{4}$ **to 1 Pint Rum**
$\frac{3}{4}$ **to 1 Pint Brandy**
1 Liqueur Glass Curacao, Noyau or Maraschino Liqueur
3-$\frac{1}{2}$ Pints Boiling Water
Juice of 3 or 4 Orange
Peel of 1 or 2 Oranges
$\frac{3}{4}$ **Pound Sugar**

Add the juice of 3 or 4 oranges and the peel of 1 or two oranges to $\frac{3}{4}$ pound of sugar and 3-$\frac{1}{2}$ pints of boiling water. Infuse [allow to sit] for half an hour, strain and add $\frac{1}{2}$ pint of porter, and $\frac{3}{4}$ to 1 pint each rum and brandy (or 1-$\frac{1}{2}$ to 2 pints rum or brandy alone). Add more warm water and sugar if desired weaker or sweeter. A liqueur glass of Curacao, noyau or maraschino improves it. A good lemon punch may be made by substituting lemons instead of oranges.

Bon-Vivant's Companion, 1862

162
Orgeat Punch
(Use a Large Bar Glass)

1-$\frac{1}{2}$ Wine Glasses Brandy
1 Dash Port Wine
1-$\frac{1}{2}$ Tablespoons Orgeat Syrup
Juice of $\frac{1}{2}$ Lemon

Place all but the port wine in a tumbler and fill with shaved ice. Shake well, ornament with berries in season, dash with port wine, and serve with straws.

Bon-Vivant's Companion, 1862

163
Philadelphia Fish House Punch

$\frac{1}{4}$ **Pint Peach Brandy**
$\frac{1}{2}$ **Pint Cognac Brandy**
$\frac{1}{4}$ **Pint Jamaica Rum**
$\frac{1}{3}$ **Pint Lemon Juice**
$\frac{3}{4}$ **Pound White Sugar**
2-$\frac{1}{2}$ Pints Cold Water

Place the above in a punch bowl, stir well, and serve.

Bon-Vivant's Companion, 1862

164
Pineapple Punch
No. 1
(For a Party of Ten)

4 Bottles Champagne
1 Pint Jamaica Rum
1 Pint Brandy
1 Gill Curacao
Juice of 4 Lemons
4 Sliced Pineapples
Pulverized White Sugar

Put the pineapple with one pound of sugar in a glass bowl, and let them stand until the sugar is well soaked in the pineapple, then add all the other ingredients, except the champagne. Let this mixture stand in ice for about an hour, then add the champagne. Place a large block of ice in the center of the bowl and ornament it with loaf sugar, sliced orange, and other fruits in season. Serve in champagne glasses.

Bon-Vivant's Companion, 1862

165
Port Wine Punch

1 Bottle Port Wine
1 Liqueur Glass Maraschino
1 Bottle Soda Water
4 Tablespoons Powdered White Sugar
3 or 4 Slices Cucumber Rind
¼ Teaspoon Grated Nutmeg
½ Pounds Ice

Put all the ingredients into a bowl or pitcher and mix well.
Ornament with berries in season.

Bon-Vivant's Companion, 1862

166
Porter Cup

1 Bottle Porter
1 Bottle Table Ale
1 Wine Glass Brandy
1 Dessertspoon Ginger Syrup
4 Lumps Sugar
½ Grated Nutmeg

Mix in a tankard or covered jug the porter and table ale,
pour in the brandy and ginger syrup, and add the sugar and
grated nutmeg. Cover it down, and expose it to the cold for
half an hour. Just before sending it to the table, stir in a
teaspoon of carbonate of soda. Add the fresh cut rind of a
cucumber.

Bon-Vivant's Companion, 1862

167
Protestant Bishop

1 Bottle Claret
4 Tablespoons Santa Cruz or Jamaica Rum
2 Tumblers Water
1 Sliced Lemon
4 Tablespoons White Sugar

Dissolve the sugar in the water, add it and the remaining ingredients to a punch bowl, mix well and add ice.

Bon-Vivant's Companion, 1862

168
Raspberry Punch

$^{1}/_{2}$ Pint Porter
1 Pint Rum
1 Pint Brandy
1 Liqueur Glass Curacao, Noyau, or Maraschino
1-$^{1}/_{2}$ Gills Raspberry Juice
$^{3}/_{4}$ Pound Lump Sugar
3-$^{1}/_{2}$ Pints Boiling Water

Infuse for half an hour the raspberry juice, sugar, and boiling water, then add the liquor. If sweeter taste is desired add more warm water and sugar.

Bon-Vivant's Companion, 1862

169
Raspberry Shrub

Brandy
1 Quart of Vinegar
3 Quarts Ripe Raspberries

Combine the vinegar and raspberries and allow to stand one day. Strain, discard the raspberry hulls, and conserve the liquid. Add to each pint of liquid one pound of sugar, and skim it clear, while boiling about half an hour. Put a wine glass of brandy to each pint of the shrub, when cool. Two spoons of this mixed with a tumbler of water, is an excellent drink in warm weather, and in fevers.

Bon-Vivant's Companion, 1862

170
Regent's Punch
(For a Party of Twenty)

The ingredients for this renowned punch are:

3 Bottles Champagne
1 Bottle Hockheimer
1 Bottle Curacao
1 Bottle Cognac
½ Bottle Jamaica Rum
2 Bottles Madeira
2 Bottles Soda or Seltzer Water
4 Pounds Bloom Raisins

Add to the above oranges, lemons, rock candy, and instead of water, green tea to taste. Refrigerate with all the icy power of the Arctic.

Bon-Vivant's Companion, 1862

171
Rochester Punch

2 Bottles Sparkling Catawba Wine
2 Bottles Sparkling Isabella Wine
1 Bottle Sauterne
2 Wine Glasses Maraschino
2 Wine Glasses Curacao

Fill the tranquil bowl with ripe strawberries and add the above. Should the strawberry season be over, or under, add a few drops of extract of peach or vanilla.

Bon-Vivant's Companion, 1862

172
Rocky Mountain Punch

This delicious punch is compounded as follows:

5 Bottles Champagne
1 Quart Jamaica Rum
1 Pint Maraschino
6 Slice Lemons
Sugar to Taste

Mix the above ingredients in a large punch bowl, then place in the center of the bowl a large square block of ice, ornament it on top with rock candy, loaf sugar, sliced lemons or oranges and fruits in season. This is a splendid punch for New Year's Day.

Bon-Vivant's Companion, 1862

173
Roman Punch

1 Wine Glass Jamaica Rum
½ Wine Glass Brandy
1 Teaspoon Curacao
1 Tablespoon Raspberry Syrup
Juice of ½ Lemon
1 Tablespoon Sugar

Fill a glass with shaved ice, shake well, dash with port wine, and ornament with fruits in season. Imbibe through a straw. [A wonderful group punch can be made by increasing the ingredients above by the number of portions required.]

Bon-Vivant's Companion, 1862

174
Royal Punch

½ **Pint Brandy**
½ **Pint Jamaica Rum**
1 Wine Glass Curacao
1 Wine Glass Arrack
1 Pint Hot Green Tea
Juice of 2 Limes
1 Gill Warm Calf's Foot Jelly
1 Thin Slice Lemon

Mix the above and drink as hot as possible. This is a composition worthy of a king, and the materials are admirably blended. The inebriating effects of the spirits are deadened by the tea, whilst the jelly softens the mixture, and destroys the acrimony of the acid and sugar. The whites of a couple of eggs well beat up to a froth, may be substituted for the jelly where that is not at hand. If the punch is too strong, add more green tea to taste.

Bon-Vivant's Companion, 1862

175
Ruby Punch

1 Pint Arrack
1 Pint Port Wine
3 Pints Hot Tea
Juice of Six Lemons
1 Pound Sugar

Dissolve one pound of sugar in three pints of hot tea. Add the juice of six lemons, a pint of arrack and a pint of port wine.

Bon-Vivant's Companion, 1862

176
Rum Shrub
(Mix in a Small Wooden Cask)

1 Gallon of Rum
3 Pints of Orange Juice
1 Pound of Loaf Sugar

Put three pints of orange juice, and one pound of loaf-sugar to a gallon of rum. Put all into a cask, and leave it for six weeks, when it will be ready for use.

Bon-Vivant's Companion, 1862

177
Rum Shrub - English
(Use a Five Gallon Bowl)

3 Gallons Jamaica Rum
1 Quart Orange Juice
6 Pounds of Powdered White Sugar
1 Pint of Lemon Juice—Save the Peels

To three gallons of best Jamaica rum, add a quart of orange juice, a pint of lemon juice, with the peels of the latter fruit cut very thin, and six pounds of powdered white sugar.

Let these be covered close, and remain so all night; next day boil three pints of fresh milk, and let it get cold, then pour it on the spirit and juice, mix them well, and let it stand for an hour. Filter through a flannel bag lined with blotting-paper, into bottles; cork down as soon as each is filled.

Bon-Vivant's Companion, 1862

178
Sauterne Punch

1 Bottle Sauterne
1 Liqueur Glass Maraschino

1 Bottle Soda Water
4 Tablespoons Powdered White Sugar
3 or 4 Slices Cucumber Rind
1/4 Teaspoon Grated Nutmeg
1/2 Pound Ice

Put all the ingredients into a bowl or pitcher and mix well.

Bon-Vivant's Companion, 1862

179
Sherry Punch
(Use a Large Bar Glass)

2 Wine Glasses Sherry
2 or 3 Orange Slices
2 or 3 Lemon Slices
1 Tablespoon Sugar

Fill a tumbler with shaved ice, shake well, and ornament with berries in season. Sip through a straw.

Bon-Vivant's Companion, 1862

180
69th Regiment Punch

1/2 Wine Glass Irish Whiskey
1/2 Wine Glass Scotch Whisky
1 Teaspoon Sugar
1 Piece of Lemon
2 Wine Glasses Hot Water

Mix the above in an earthen mug and serve while hot. This is capital punch for a cold night.

Bon-Vivant's Companion, 1862

181
Spread Eagle Punch

1 Bottle Islay Whiskey
1 Bottle Monongahela (Rye) Whiskey
Lemon Peel
Boiling Water
Sugar

Add the whiskey to the lemon peel, sugar, and water, the latter at your discretion.

Bon-Vivant's Companion, 1862

182
St. Charles' Punch
(Use a Large Bar Glass)

1 Wine Glass Port Wine
1 Pony Brandy
Juice of $\frac{1}{4}$ Lemon
1 Tablespoon Sugar

Fill the tumbler with shaved ice, shake well, and ornament with fruits in season, and serve with a straw.

Bon-Vivant's Companion, 1862

183
Tea Punch

½ Pint Good Brandy
½ Pint Good Rum
¼ Pound Lump Sugar
Green Tea
Boiling Water
Juice of 1 Large Lemon

Make an infusion of the best green tea, an ounce to a quart of boiling water; put before the fire a silver or other metal bowl, to become quite hot, and then put into it the brandy, rum, sugar and lemon juice. Set these alight, and pour in the tea gradually, mixing it from time to time with a ladle. It will remain burning for some time and it is to be poured in that state into the glasses. In order to increase the flavor, a few lumps of sugar should be rubbed over the lemon peel. This punch may be made in a china bowl, but in that case the flame goes off more rapidly.

Bon-Vivant's Companion, 1862

184
32nd Regiment or Victoria Punch
(for a Party of Twenty)

½ Gallon Brandy
½ Gallon Jamaica Rum
1 Pint Boiling Milk
1-¾ Quart Water
1 Pound White Sugar

Steep the lemons for 24 hours in the brandy and rum. Add the sugar, water and milk, and when well mixed, strain through a jelly bag. This punch may be bottled, and used afterward hot or cold. Half the above quantity, or even less, may be made, as this recipe is for a party of twenty.

Bon-Vivant's Companion, 1862

185
Tip-Top Punch
(For a Party of Five)

1 Bottle Champagne
2 Bottles Soda Water
1 Liqueur Glass Curacao
2 Tablespoons Powdered Sugar
1 Sliced Pineapple

Put all the ingredients together in a small punch bowl, mix well, and serve in champagne goblets.

Bon-Vivant's Companion, 1862

186
Tom and Jerry

$\frac{1}{2}$ Wine Glass Jamaica Rum
12 Eggs
5 Pounds Sugar
1-$\frac{1}{2}$ Teaspoons Ground Cinnamon
$\frac{1}{2}$ Teaspoon Ground Cloves
$\frac{1}{2}$ Teaspoon Ground Allspice

In a punch bowl, beat the whites of the eggs to a stiff froth, and the yolks they are as thin as water, then mix together and add the spice and rum. Thicken with sugar until the mixture attains the consistency of a light batter.

To deal out Tom and Jerry to customers:

Take a small bar glass, and to one tablespoon of the above mixture, add one wine glass of brandy, and fill the glass with boiling water, grate a little nutmeg on top.

Adepts at the bar, in serving Tom and Jerry, sometimes adopt a mixture of one-half brandy, one-quarter wine glass Jamaica rum and one-quarter Santa Cruz rum instead of plain brandy. This compound is usually mixed and kept in a bottle, and a wine glass is used to each tumbler of Tom and Jerry.

A teaspoon of cream of tartar, or about as much carbonate of soda as you can get on a dime will prevent the sugar from settling to the bottom of the mixture.

This drink is sometimes called Copenhagen, and sometimes Jerry Thomas.

Bon-Vivant's Companion, 1862

187
Trinidad Punch

1 Pint Rum
2 Pints Coconut Milk
1 Ounce Chocolate
½ Stick Vanilla

Digest the chocolate and vanilla in the rum, strain into a small punch bowl when well incorporated, and add the coconut milk. This punch can be used either as a cool cup, with ice, or hot.

Cooling Cups and Dainty Drinks, 1869

188
'Tween Deck Cup
or
A Splitting Headache

2 Quarts Bottled Ale
¼ Pint Rum
¼ Pint Lime Juice
6 Crushed Cloves
Cinnamon
Ginger
Nutmeg

Into one-quarter pint of rum, put six crushed cloves and a little cinnamon, nutmeg and ginger. Strain in an hour, with pressure, add an equal quantity of lime juice and two quarts of bottled ale.

Cooling Cups and Dainty Drinks, 1869

189
United Service Punch

1 Pint Arrack
2 Pints Hot Tea
¾ Pound Loaf Sugar
Peels of 4 Lemons
Juice of 8 Lemons

Dissolve three-quarters of a pound of loaf sugar in two pints of hot tea, having previously rubbed the sugar on the peels of four lemons. Add the lemon juice and a pint of arrack.

Bon-Vivant's Companion, 1862

190
The University Punch

1 Pint Cognac
1 Pint Old Rum
3 Wine Glasses Curacao or Orange Brandy
1 Pint Capillaire
3 Wine Glasses Sherry
7 Fresh Lemons
Lump Sugar
3 Wine Glasses Curacao or Orange Brandy
3 Seville Oranges
1 Pot Red Currant or Guava Jelly

Take six fresh lemons, rub the rinds on loaf sugar until you have absorbed all the yellow part. Add the lemon juice, the peel and juice of the oranges, and a pot of red currant or guava jelly. Place mixture in an earthen jug, pour in one pint of boiling water and stand the jug in a pan of boiling water. Add the cognac, rum, capillaire, Curacao or orange brandy, and sherry. Let the mixture stand for twenty minutes, strain off, and add three pints of boiling water and the peel of a lemon cut thinly.

Gentleman's Table Guide, 1873

191
Vanilla Punch
(Use a Large Bar Glass)

1 Wine Glass Brandy
Juice of ¼ Lemon
2 Lemon Slices
Vanilla Extract
1 Tablespoon Sugar

Add the sugar, brandy and lemon juice to a tumbler and fill with shaved ice. Shake well, ornament with one or two lemon slices, and flavor with a few drops of vanilla extract.

This is a delicious drink and should be imbibed through a glass tube or straw.

Bon-Vivant's Companion, 1862

On Whiskey Punches Served Cold ...

[Whiskey punches served cold] ought always to be made with boiling water, and allowed to concoct and cool for a day or two before they are put on the table. In this way the materials get more intensely amalgamated than cold water and cold whiskey every get.

Note: Irish whiskey is not fit to drink until it is three years old. The best whiskey for this purpose is Kenahan's LL Whiskey.

–Jerry Thomas

192
Irish Whiskey Punch

$\frac{1}{3}$ **Pure Irish Whiskey**
$\frac{2}{3}$ **Boiling Water**
Sugar to Taste
Lemon Rind and Juice to Taste

This is the genuine Irish beverage. It is generally made one-third pure whiskey, two-thirds boiling water, in which the sugar has been dissolved. If lemon punch, the rind is rubbed on the sugar, and a small proportion of juice added before the whiskey is poured in.

If served cold, allow to concoct and cool for a day or two before putting on the table. Then ice and imbibe.

Bon-Vivant's Companion, 1862

193
Scotch Whiskey Punch

Glenlivet or Islay Whiskey
Shavings of Lemon Peel
Sugar

As it requires genius to make whiskey punch, it would be impertinent to give proportions.

Steep the thin yellow shavings of lemon peel in the whiskey, which should be Glenlivet of Islay, of the best quality; the sugar should be dissolved in boiling water.

If served cold, allow to concoct and cool for a day or two before putting on the table. Then ice and imbibe.

Bon-Vivant's Companion, 1862

194
White Currant Shrub
(Use a One Gallon Bowl)

1 Gallon of Rum
2 Quarts of Currants
2 Pounds of Lump-Sugar

Strip the fruit, and prepare in a jar, as for jelly. Strain the juice, of which put two quarts to one gallon of rum, and two pounds of lump-sugar. Strain through a jelly-bag.

Bon-Vivant's Companion, 1862

195
Yankee Punch

1 Pint Brandy
1 Bottle Claret
½ Bottle Port Wine
1 Pint Lemon Juice
1 Pint Lemon Syrup
8 Drops Essence of Vanilla
1 Dessert Spoon of Orange Flower Water
2 Lumps Sugar
Water

Drop on each of the two lumps of sugar the essence of vanilla. Put into a bottle containing one pint of brandy and when well digested add the lemon juice, lemon syrup, port wine, claret, and orange flower water. Mix, sweeten according to taste, and add as much water as required.

Cooling Cups and Dainty Drinks, 1869

Sangarees

Sangaree is an English corruption of the Spanish term *Sangria*, a punch-like concoction made of Madeira wine, lime juice, sugar and nutmeg served at room temperature. The Spanish term is a derivative of *sangre*, meaning blood, in reference to the red wine color of the drink. Written references to Sangaree date back to 1736, and it was said to have been the most popular beverage in the Spanish Caribbean Islands. British and American sailors picked up the drink and popularized it in the American colonies.

Nineteenth-century bartenders changed the recipes and methods of serving considerably. Sangarees became single-portion drinks, usually iced, with a red wine, ale, whiskey or brandy base. The liquor of choice was mixed with water and sugar, and the finished drink was garnished with nutmeg and fruit slices. Most recipes omitted fruit juice, but a few included Curacao to impart a strong orange taste.

In recent years sangria wine has become a big seller among persons looking for an alternative to hard liquors. The mixture of red wine, sugar and citrus fruits is not unlike some 18th century red wine Sangarees.

Ale Sangaree
See Ale and Beer Drinks

196
Brandy Sangaree
(Use a Small Bar Glass)

1 Wine Glass Brandy
$\frac{1}{2}$ Wine Glass Water
1 Teaspoon Port Wine
1 Teaspoon Sugar

Dissolve the sugar in a little water. Fill the glass $\frac{2}{3}$ full of shaved ice, shake up well, strain into a small glass and dash a little port wine so that it will float on top.

Bon-Vivant's Companion, 1862

197
Gin Sangaree

Make the same as a Brandy Sangaree, but substitute gin for brandy.

Bon-Vivant's Companion, 1862

198
Port Wine Sangaree
(Use a Small Bar Glass)

1-$\frac{1}{2}$ Wine Glasses Port Wine
1 Teaspoon Sugar
A Little Nutmeg

Take one-half teaspoonful of fine white sugar and dissolve in a little water. Fill tumbler two-thirds full of ice, add the dissolved sugar and port wine, shake well, strain into a small bar glass, grate a little nutmeg on top, and serve. [Slices of a peeled lemon are added to some versions of the Port Wine Sangaree after mixing.]

Bon-Vivant's Companion, 1862

199
Sherry Sangaree

$\frac{1}{2}$ Pint Brown Sherry
2 Tablespoons Powdered Sugar
1 Slice Pineapple
A Little Nutmeg

Dissolve two tablespoonfuls powdered sugar in a wine glass full of water. Add this and one-half pint of brown sherry to a large tumbler two-thirds full of pounded ice. Stir, strain into a large bar glass and ornament with a slice of pineapple and a little grated nutmeg. Serve with straws. Also called Port or Sherry Cobbler or Sangaree.

Cooling Cups and Dainty Drinks, 1869

Sours

Fancy Brandy Sour.

Sours have been mentioned in print since the 1850s. Brandy and Gin sours are the first recorded, followed in the 1870s by sours containing rum and whiskey. The common element in every sour is a healthy dose of lemon juice.

200
Brandy Sour
(Use a Small Bar Glass)

1 Wine Glass Brandy
$\frac{1}{2}$ Wine Glass Water
Juice of $\frac{1}{4}$ Lemon
1 Tablespoon Sugar

Fill a tumbler two-thirds full of shaved ice and add the above ingredients. Stir with a spoon and serve.

Bon-Vivant's Companion, 1862

201
Gin Sour
(Use a Small Bar Glass)

1 Wine Glass Gin
$\frac{1}{2}$ Wine Glass Water
Juice of $\frac{1}{4}$ Lemon
1 Tablespoon Sugar

Take one large teaspoon of white sugar dissolved in a little seltzer or Appolinaris water. Fill a tumbler full of shaved ice, add the above ingredients and shake up well. Strain into a claret glass. Dress the top with orange, or pineapple and berries.

Bon-Vivant's Companion, 1862

Toddys and Slings

Soldiers of the far flung British empire were responsible for adding the word "toddy" to the lexicon of drinks. While serving in 18th century India they encountered palm liquors called *tari tadi* in Hindu. When the stems of various Middle Eastern, Asian and Caribbean palms are punctured, they produce a sweet juice that will readily ferment into a potent, whitish liquor. This fact had been known to natives of these areas for thousands of years.

Glowing accounts of *tadi* by returning soldiers, coupled with the scarcity of palm trees in Great Britain, led to poor imitations of palm liquor. Fermented palm juice was replaced with rum, whiskey, applejack, gin and brandy sweetened with sugar and spiced with nutmeg. Eventually *tadi* was corrupted to *toddy*, and the basic recipe became spirits, sugar, water and lemon peel. Hot and cold toddy spread to the American colonies by 1790, where it was enthusiastically embraced by upper and lower class tipplers.

The best known toddy is the Apple Toddy, which features a baked apple fortified with brandy or whiskey. Many saloon hot water urns were fitted with apple roasters on top to supply the roast "pippins" needed for apple toddy recipes.

The Sling can be traced back to 1807 in America. It was once thought to be a drink of American invention, but the term is a corruption of the German *schlingen*, meaning "to drink." Originally there was but one kind of sling, made from gin, bitters, lemon juice, ice and sugar. Later other types of liquor, fruit and spices were used, and then sparkling water was added. Hot slings, developed after the 1860s, were so similar to toddys that many bartenders' guides left out slings altogether.

Slings, in their 1860s forms, were almost similar to toddys. Jerry Thomas wrote, "Brandy, gin and whiskey Slings are made with the same ingredients as Toddys, except you grate a little nutmeg on top."

202
Apple Toddy
No. 1
(Use a Small Bar Glass)

1 Wine Glass Applejack
½ Baked Apple
1 Tablespoon Fine White Sugar

Fill the glass two-thirds full of boiling water, add the above ingredients, and grate a little nutmeg on top.

Bon-Vivant's Companion, 1862

203
Apple Toddy
No. 2

1 Gill Brandy
½ Pint Boiling Cider
1 Ounce Powdered Sugar
1 Baked Apple

Put a baked apple in a glass; add one ounce of powdered sugar, one gill of brandy, one-half pint of boiling cider; grate a little ginger on top of the liquor; ornament with a piece of lemon peel.

Cooling Cups and Dainty Drinks, 1869

204
Apple Toddy
No. 3
(Use a Tumbler)

1 Wine Glass Peach or Orange Brandy
½ Baked Apple
1 Tablespoon Powdered Rock Candy or Sugar

Combine one tablespoon of powdered sugar or rock candy with one wine glass peach or orange brandy. Add one-half a baked apple, fill the glass two-thirds full of boiling water, and place a little grated nutmeg on top.

Gentleman's Table Guide, 1873

205
Brandy Toddy
(Use a Small Bar Glass)

½ Wine Glass Brandy
½ Wine Glass Water
1 Teaspoonful Sugar

Combine the above and a lump of ice in a small bar glass. Stir with a spoon. For a hot brandy toddy omit the ice, and use boiling water.

Bon-Vivant's Companion, 1862

206
Gin Toddy

Same as Brandy Toddy No. 1, except substitute gin for brandy.

Bon-Vivant's Companion, 1862

207
Whiskey Toddy

Same as Brandy Toddy No. 1, except substitute rye whiskey for brandy.

Bon-Vivant's Companion, 1862

208
Whiskey Sling

$\frac{1}{4}$ **Pint Gin or Whiskey**
Thin Peel of an Orange
Juice of 2 Oranges and 1 Lemon
Sugar

Soak the thin peel of an orange or lemon in one-quarter pint
of gin or whiskey. Add the juice of two oranges and one
lemon; sugar to taste; add one pint of pounded lake ice;
serve with straws.

Bon-Vivant's Companion, 1862
Cooling Cups and Dainty Drinks, 1869

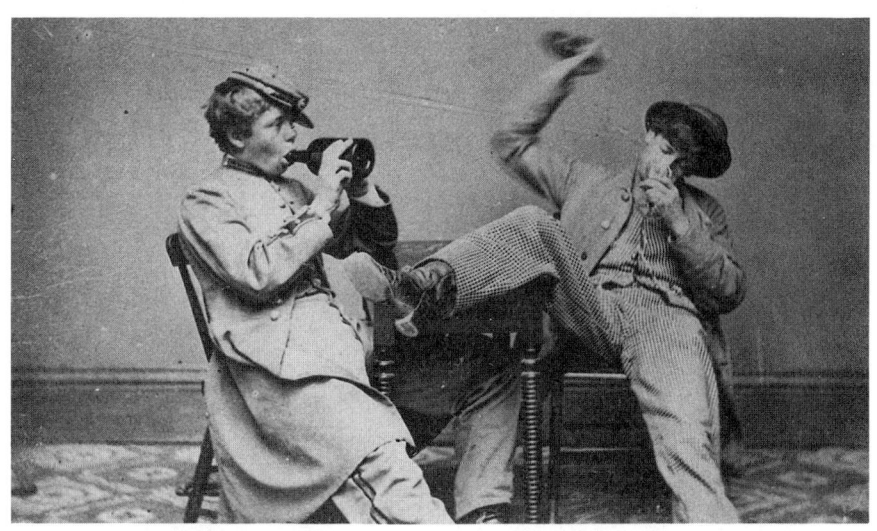

*"Over the Bay" was number three of the five-part series probably staged by H.
Skinner in 1862. (William Welling)*

The Manufacture
of Liquors

The quality of liquor in the 1860s and '70s was often "questionable," but few minded if it inebriated.

Enterprising drinkers and businessmen make their own spirits whenever supplies of brewed and distilled liquors become scarce or expensive. This was true when the Confederacy prohibited the manufacture of liquors to preserve foodstuffs. It was true in the winter camps of the Union army when drinking was prohibited. It was true when sutlers wanted to increase their profit margins by manufacturing their own stock. And it was true in saloons on the western frontier where champagne, whiskey and cordials were often unavailable.

Two types of manuals were available to guide the uninitiated in the manufacture of brewed and distilled liquors. This chapter quotes "safe" recipes from Christian Schlutz' *Manual for the Manufacture of Cordials, Liquors, Fancy Syrups, &c. &c.*

By using hops, yeast, various essences, oils and flavorings one could produce either the real thing, or a passable imitation of beer, ale, gin and rum. Where imitation was not possible, or advisable, Schultz' provided instructions on how to dilute the real article with grain alcohol or lesser quality whiskey and wine.

Today's sophisticated drinkers will find little to praise in the following recipes. However, unlike Pierre Lacour's recipes in the following chapter, most of these recipes will not make you ill if consumed in reasonable amounts.

We do recommend avoiding recipe 212, which requires oil of turpentine. Please see the **Glossary** for information on other ingredients.

209
Ale
(About 8 Gallons)

2 Gallons Ground Malt
6 Gallons of Water at 142° degrees F
2 Ounces Hops

Stir the malt and water together; let it stand for 1-½ hours, draw off the liquid as much as possible. Repeat the operation with 3 gallons more of the same warm water, and the same standing. Draw off the liquor again, and repeat the third time with 3 gallons more, as before; mix the liquors together and boil them with 2 ounces of hops. Clarify the whole with the white of an egg, filter while hot, cool as quickly as possible, stir in $\frac{1}{2}$ pound of yeast, and let it ferment.

Manual for the Manufacture of Cordials, 1862

210
Hop Beer
(About 10 Gallons)

10 Gallons of Water
2 Ounces of Hops
16 Pounds Sugar
1-$\frac{1}{2}$ Pint Brewers Yeast

Boil 2 ounces of hops for 10 minutes in 10 gallons of water with 16 pounds of sugar. Then skim and strain; let it cool to 80° degrees F. Add 1-$\frac{1}{2}$ pints of brewers' yeast and let it stand for 24 hours. Filter, and fill it in an iron-bound and well pitched cask, and bung it up tight.

Manual for the Manufacture of Cordials, 1862

211
Domestic Gin
(About 10 Gallons)

5-$\frac{1}{4}$ Gallons 190 Proof Alcohol
4-$\frac{5}{8}$ Gallons Water
$\frac{1}{2}$ Gallon White Plain Syrup
3 Drams Oil of Juniper

Dissolve oil of Juniper in the alcohol, then add the water and plain syrup.

Manual for the Manufacture of Cordials, 1862

212
English Gin
(About 10 Gallons)

5-$\frac{1}{4}$ Gallons 190 Proof Alcohol
4-$\frac{3}{4}$ Gallons Water
3 Drams Oil of Juniper
1 Drams Oil of Turpentine

Dissolve the oils of Juniper and Turpentine in the alcohol, then add the water.

Manual for the Manufacture of Cordials, 1862

213
Holland Gin
(About 10 Gallons)

2-$\frac{1}{2}$ Gallons Holland Gin
3-$\frac{3}{4}$ Gallons 190 Proof Alcohol
3-$\frac{3}{4}$ Gallons Water

Manual for the Manufacture of Cordials, 1862

214
Jamaica Rum
(About 10 Gallons)

7 Pounds Fragments of Sugar Cane
6 Gallons of 190 Proof Alcohol
4 Gallons of Water
13 Ounces Common Salt

Soak 7 pounds of sugar cane fragments in 6 gallons of 95% alcohol and 4 gallons of water. Add the salt and distill 6 gallons of flavored spirit. Add 3-$\frac{1}{2}$ gallons of water and $\frac{1}{4}$ gallon of plain syrup. Color dark yellow with oak bark.

Manual for the Manufacture of Cordials, 1862

215
St. Croix Rum
(About 40 Gallons)

Dissolve 62 pounds of brown sugar in 40 gallons of boiling water. Cool it down to 80° degrees F. Add 1 gallon of brewer's yeast. When fermentation is over, distill.

Manual for the Manufacture of Cordials, 1862

Whiskey

Without large distilleries these whiskeys—Irish and Scotch—cannot be manufactured with profit. It is a humbug to make them with essences and a nuisance as regards health. The best imitation is mixing in proportion to the price.

—Christian Schultz

216
Irish Whiskey
(About 10 Gallons)

3 Gallons of Genuine Irish Whiskey
7 Gallons 190 Proof Alcohol

Manual for the Manufacture of Cordials, 1862

217
Monongahela Whiskey
(About 10 Gallons)

3 Gallons of Monongahela Whiskey
7 Gallons 190 Proof Alcohol

Color Yellow with Saffron Mixture.

Manual for the Manufacture of Cordials, 1862

218
Scotch Whiskey
(About 10 Gallons)

3 Gallons of Best Genuine Scotch Whiskey
7 Gallons 190 Proof Alcohol

Manual for the Manufacture of Cordials, 1862

219
Red Bordeaux Wine
(About 10 Gallons)

4 Gallons High Flavored Red Bordeaux Wine
6 Gallons Plain Red Wine

Color to the same shade of red as the Bordeaux wine with Tincture of Alderberries.

Manual for the Manufacture of Cordials, 1862

220
White Bordeaux Wine
(About 10 Gallons)

4 Gallons High Flavored White Bordeaux Wine
6 Gallons Plain White Wine

Color to the same shade of white as the Bordeaux wine with Tincture of Saffron.

Manual for the Manufacture of Cordials, 1862

221
Champagne
(About 10 Gallons)

10 Gallons Rhine or Sauterne Wine
3 Pounds Rock Candy Dissolved in 1-$\frac{1}{2}$ Pints Water
$\frac{1}{2}$ Gallon 190 Proof Alcohol
1-$\frac{1}{2}$ Drams of Citric Acid
1-$\frac{1}{2}$ Drams of Bicarbonate of Soda

Bottle, cork, wire, cap and label.

Manual for the Manufacture of Cordials, 1862

"Going Home" was the fourth of the five Skinner photos. (William Welling)

A Humbug
and a Nuisance
as Regards Health

Throughout the war unscrupulous liquorists and sutlers sold scurrilous imitation liquors to unsuspecting soldiers and civilians. These spirits were usually based on raw alcohol, acids, creosote, ethers, and turpentine. "Kick" was furnished by ammonia, astringents, pepper solutions and sulfuric acid or vinegar.

Soldiers from the farm and the ghetto who had never tasted real champagne or Cognac were amazed to find they could buy it from a sutler. Unknown to them, they were buying adulterated grain alcohol instead of the genuine articles. Since their goal was often a prolonged drunk, they did not care as long as it had a manly bite and produced rapid inebriation.

We can gain a glimpse of this illicit trade through Pierre Lacour's 1852 book *The Manufacture of Liquors, Wines and Cordials, without the Aid of Distillation.* It was a profiteer's guide that instructed con men on how to make liquors seem strong without using too much expensive alcohol:

> The burning sensation produced by pepper and alcohol is nearly identical; and it must be obvious that the former will answer all the purposes of the latter, with the exception of not furnishing the intoxicating quality, which must be added in the form of alcohol. In the manufacture of all the cheap light wines, cordials, &c. where alcohol would be an important consideration, pecuniarily, Guinea pepper will answer admirably.

The recipes were unconscionable frauds, as can be seen by this recipe for increasing the amount of whiskey on hand:

Rectified Whiskey

20 Gallons Raw Whiskey
20 Gallons Water
1-$\frac{1}{2}$ Gallons Tincture Guinea Pepper
1 Pint Tincture Pellitory
3 Quarts Strong Decoction Samqua Tea

Put on a bead of oil and acid, add 1-1/2 pint sugar coloring and tumbler of tincture of Red Sanders Wood [Sandalwood coloring].

Lacour used tea, pellitory (a throat-closing astringent), pepper water and Sandalwood coloring to stretch supplies of the genuine article. His formula for adding a bead to beer, ale or other drinks was 20 Drops of Sulfuric Acid and 30 drops of sweet oil. Sweet oil, or essence of saltpeter, was a distillate of nitric acid and alcohol. Lacour admitted that sweet oil would "cause an involuntary flow of urine from the consumer."

When it came to selling fake ale, beer and porter, Lacour advised purchasing fake labels modeled on real brands. He also recommended that his students sell their items at auction, no doubt to shirk later repercussions from outraged consumers.

> It may be necessary to state for the benefit of the uninitiated reader when and how this kind of porter and ale is disposed of to form a remunerative investment (sic).
>
> This consists in bottling and labelling this Fluid with neatness. The labels should be obtained from the lithographers, and should be executed in the highest style of the art. The same articles are sold under the names of London porter; and the ale receives all the names of the different varieties of that article, that have acquired any celebrity in commerce, such as Scotch ale, Indian pale ale, pineapple ale &c., &c. The bottles are packed in barrels or boxes, and are disposed of at auction. This ale is usually manufactured at cost varying from four to eight cents per gallon.

All of this fraud and fakery was to have an impact on the liquor industry for years to come. One of the primary weapons used by the Anti-Saloon movement of the 1890s was the harmful effects of these fake liquors on consumers.

Do not make or consume these recipes. They are included solely for historical interest.

222
Cheap Ale

Boil two pounds of wheaten flour well worked into a paste, with ten pounds of brown sugar, and one pound of hops; six ounces of ground cinnamon, three ounces of braised ginger, six ounces of grains of paradise ground, two ounces of quassia, in twelve gallons of water for forty minutes; when near cold, add one and a half pints of yeast. Ferment until it quits frothing, then strain through flannel; add eight ounces of ether, and then bottle.

Manufacture of Liquors, 1853

223
Cheap Porter for Bottling

Boil a peck of wheat bran for one hour, together with one pound of hops, in twelve gallons of water, and while warm strain through flannel, to separate the bran from the liquor. Then stir in one gallon of molasses, one fourth of a pint of burnt sugar, one and a half pints of yeast, and once ounce of powdered aloes. Set the vessel aside in a warm place to ferment. This will be known by the froth that arises to the surface of the liquor. This should be skimmed off when the froth ceases to rise to the surface. It should be bottled. If this is for immediate use, say within six weeks, add a lump of sugar, and a teaspoonful of yeast to every bottle before filling.

Manufacture of Liquors, 1853

224
Apple Brandy
(About 40 Gallons)

Apple brandy belongs to that class of liquors that pays but a small percentage, and, therefore, is scarcely worth noticing. A cheap [imitation] of this brandy is made of

40 Gallons Distilled Whiskey 80 to 90 Proof
8 Ounces Acetic Acid
1 Ounce Sulfuric Acid
3 Sliced Red Beets
1 Pint Burnt Sugar Coloring

Allow the above to stand in a barrel for 10 days with one pint of wheat or rice flour, slightly scorched, suspended in the barrel inside a muslin bag.

Manufacture of Liquors, 1853

225
Cognac Brandy
(About 112 Gallons)

40 Gallons 80 to 140 Proof Alcohol
35 Gallons Water
1 Gallon Strong Tea
1 Gallon Tincture of Grains of Paradise
20 Pounds Sugar Dissolved in 35 Gallons Water
2 Quarts Prune Spirit
3 Ounces Acetic Ether
1 Quart Burnt Sugar Coloring
1 Pint Tincture of Sanders Wood Coloring

This is strong brandy.

Manufacture of Liquors, 1853

226
Cognac Brandy
(5 Gallons)

4 Gallons 80 to 140 Proof Alcohol
½ Gallon Honey Dissolved in 2 Pints Water
1 Gallon Jamaica Rum
½ Ounce Catechu
1 Ounce Butyric Ether

Manufacture of Liquors, 1853

227
Cognac Brandy
(5 Gallons)

4 Gallons 80 to 140 Proof Alcohol
5 Pounds of Sugar Dissolved in 4 Pints of Water
2 Pints of Tea
1 Pint Infusion of Bitter Almonds
1 Ounce Oil of Wine
5 Ounces Tincture of Cochineal
9 Ounces Burnt Sugar Coloring

Manufacture of Liquors, 1853

228
New York Brandy
(About 72 Gallons)

30 Gallons 80 to 140 Proof Alcohol
40 Gallons Water
2 Gallons Tincture of Grains of Paradise
2 Ounces Nitric Ether
3 Ounces Acetic Ether
1 Ounce Sulfuric Acid
Color with Red Beets and Burnt Sugar

Manufacture of Liquors, 1853

229
Peach Brandy
(130 Gallons)

70 Gallons 80 to 140 Proof Alcohol
5 Gallons Honey Dissolved in 55 Gallons Water
1-$\frac{1}{2}$ Ounces English Saffron
15 Drops Creosote
$\frac{1}{2}$ Ounce Balsam of Peru

1 Wine Glass Essence of Lemon
½ Ounce Essence of Orange Peel

In America, almost everyone is acquainted with peach brandy. The above recipe furnishes a really fine sample of "old peach." It will have a fine body, pleasant taste and approved flavor. [It is often] sold for a distilled spirit, and is branded on the head [of barrels] to the effect that it is the product of some high sounding, though imaginary, distillery.

Manufacture of Liquors, 1853

230
English Gin
(About 108 Gallons)

100 Gallons 80 to 140 Proof Alcohol
3 Gallons Honey & 20 Pounds Sugar Dissolved in
5 Gallons Water
2 Ounces Oil of Juniper Dissolved in a Few Ounces Alcohol
6 Ounces Spirit of Vanilla
1 Pounds Bitter Almonds

Soak the almonds in two gallons of the spirit for 48 hours, then strain into the mix. Dissolve the oil of Juniper in the alcohol before adding to the mix.

Manufacture of Liquors, 1853

231
Holland Gin
(5 Gallons)

4 Gallons 80 to 140 Proof Alcohol
3 Pounds Sugar Dissolved in 2 Pints Water
4 Drops Strasburg Turpentine Dissolved in Alcohol
12 Drops Oil of Juniper Dissolved in Alcohol
½ Ounce Spirit of Orris Root

Manufacture of Liquors, 1853

232
Holland Gin
(100 Gallons)

100 Gallons 80 to 140 Proof Alcohol
$\frac{1}{2}$ Ounce Juniper Oil Dissolved in $\frac{1}{2}$ Glass of Alcohol
$\frac{1}{2}$ Ounce Angelic Essence

Filter 20 gallons of the clean spirit through starch, this is to give the whole mass body.

Manufacture of Liquors, 1853

233
New York Gin
(100 Gallons)

100 Gallons 80 to 90 Proof Whiskey
2 Ounces Oil of Juniper Dissolved in 3 Ounces of Alcohol
A Few Drops of Turpentine (optional)

Manufacture of Liquors, 1853

234
Cheap New York Gin
(100 Gallons)

60 Gallons Distilled 80 to 90 Proof Whiskey
30 Gallons Water
2 Gallons Tincture Grains of Paradise
$\frac{1}{2}$ Gallon Tincture of Mustard
1 Ounce Sulfuric Acid
2 Ounces Oil of Juniper Dissolved in $\frac{1}{2}$ Pint Alcohol
6 Ounces Nitric Ether
4 Ounces of Powdered Alum

The Tincture of Mustard is made by digesting 1 pound of ground mustard in half a gallon of whiskey, for 36 hours.

Manufacture of Liquors, 1853

235
Rose Gin
(100 Gallons)

100 Gallons Distilled 80 to 90 Proof Whiskey
2 Ounces Oil of Juniper Dissolved in 2 Ounces of Alcohol
12 Ounces Nitric Ether

Manufacture of Liquors, 1853

236
Schiedam Schnapps Gin - Aromatic
(About 4 Gallons)

4 Gallons 80 to 140 Proof Alcohol
4 Pints Honey Dissolved in 4 Pints Water
15 Drops Oil of Juniper Dissolved in 1 Ounce Nitric Ether

Manufacture of Liquors, 1853

237
Schiedam Swan Gin
(100 Gallons)

100 Gallons 80 to 140 Proof Alcohol
40 Pounds Refined Sugar Dissolved in 4 Gallons of Water
2 Ounces Oil of Juniper Dissolved in a Few Ounces of
   Alcohol
$\frac{1}{2}$ Oil of Coriander
4 Ounces Nitric Ether

Manufacture of Liquors, 1853

238
Jamaica Rum
(About 5 Gallons)

4 Gallons 80 to 140 Proof Alcohol
1 Gallon Jamaica Rum
$^1/_2$ Ounce Sulfuric Acid
4 Ounces Acetic Ether
8 Ounces Burnt Sugar Coloring

Manufacture of Liquors, 1853

239
Jamaica Rum
(About 122 Gallons)

100 Gallons 80 to 140 Proof Alcohol
8 to 12 Gallons Jamaica Rum
60 Pounds Sugar Dissolved in 5 Gallons Water
5 Gallons Pale Ale
2 Ounces Sulfuric Acid
8 Ounces Acetic Ether
1-$^1/_2$ Pints Burnt Sugar Coloring
$^1/_2$ Pint Tincture of Sanders Wood

Manufacture of Liquors, 1853

240
St. Croix Rum
(About 110 Gallons)

100 Gallons 80 to 140 Proof Alcohol
5 Gallons Jamaica Rum
40 Pounds of Sugar Dissolved in 5 Gallons Water
5 Ounces Catechu
1 Wine Glass Spirit of Vanilla
5 Ounces Acetic Acid

½ Gallon Tincture Grains of Paradise
1-½ Ounces Sulfuric Acid

Manufacture of Liquors, 1853

241
Old Bourbon Whiskey
(5 Gallons)

4 Gallons 80 to 140 Proof Alcohol
3 Pounds Sugar Dissolved in 3 Quarts of Water
1 Pint Decoction of Tea
3 Drops Oil of Wintergreen Dissolved in 1 Ounce Alcohol
2 Ounces Tincture Cochineal
3 Ounces Burnt Sugar

Manufacture of Liquors, 1853

242
Old Bourbon Whiskey
(126 Gallons)

100 Gallons 80 to 140 Proof Alcohol
25 Gallons Water
1 Gallon Strong Tea
1 Gallon Tincture Grains of Paradise
30 Drops of Wintergreen Oil Dissolved in 1 Ounce Alcohol

Manufacture of Liquors, 1853

243
Old Bourbon Whiskey for Bottling
(About 7 Gallons)

5 Gallons 80 to 140 Proof Alcohol
1 Gallon Honey Dissolved in ½ Gallon Water
2 Quarts Juice of Dried Peaches

1 Ounce Sulfuric Acid
$\frac{1}{2}$ Pint Spirit of Nutmegs
2 Ounces Acetic Ether
4 Drops Oil of Wintergreen Well Rubbed in Sugar
$\frac{1}{2}$ Pint of Tincture of Cochineal
$\frac{1}{2}$ Pint Burnt Sugar

Manufacture of Liquors, 1853

244
Irish Whiskey
(133 Gallons)

92 Gallons 80 to 140 Proof Alcohol
35 Gallons Water
30 Pounds Sugar Dissolved in 6 Gallons Water
30 Drops Creosote
2 Ounces Water of Ammonia

Manufacture of Liquors, 1853

245
Cheap Irish Whiskey
(About 30 Gallons)

30 Gallons Distilled 80 to 90 Proof Whiskey
3 Quarts Tincture Grains of Paradise
2 Ounces Catechu
10 Drops Creosote
5 Gallons Water

Mix the whiskey, Grains of Paradise and Water, then add the remaining ingredients. Pass through a bed composed of ground oatmeal, or of ground rice, of a mass composed of three parts of unground rice, to one part of wheat flour. This bed should be about twelve inches in depth, and for convenience can be arranged in an empty whiskey barrel.

The spirit should pass with rapidity through the filter, and if it comes off too highly charged with starch, it should have clean spirit added until the starch becomes dissipated, or is not perceptible to the naked eye; or if the spirit should be too heavy, or cloudy run through the sand filter alone until it comes out bright. The amount of flour necessary to impart the desired flavor to the spirit, is not distinguishable by the naked eye; and neither should the liquor have the slightest tinge imparted to its original color.

Manufacture of Liquors, 1853

246
Monongahela Whiskey
(5 Gallons)

4 Gallons 80 to 140 Proof Alcohol
3 Pints Honey Dissolved in 1 Gallon Water
1 Gallon Alcoholic Solution of Starch
$\frac{1}{2}$ Gallon of Rum
$\frac{1}{2}$ Ounce of Nitric Ether

Colored to suit fancy.

Manufacture of Liquors, 1853

247
Monongahela Whiskey
(About 128 Gallons)

100 Gallons Distilled 80 to 90 Proof Whiskey
25 Gallons Water
2 Gallons Decoction of Strong Tea
1 Gallon Tincture of Grains of Paradise
1 Quart Sanders Wood
1 Quart Burnt Sugar

Manufacture of Liquors, 1853

248
Monongahela Whiskey for Bottling
(About 6 Gallons)

5 Gallons 80 to 140 Proof Alcohol
½ Gallon Honey Dissolved in 1 Gallon Water
6 Ounces Bruised Bitter Almonds
1 Quart Rum
1 Ounce Catechu
50 Drops Spirit of Vanilla
½ Pint Tincture of Cochineal
½ Pint Clean Burnt Sugar

This is a superb liquor, and of fine color.

Manufacture of Liquors, 1853

249
Monongahela Rye Whiskey
(About 123 Gallons)

100 Gallons Common Whiskey
20 Gallons Water
2 Gallons Decoction of Strong Tea
1 Gallon Tincture of Grains of Paradise
2 Grains of Ambergris Dissolved in Hot Alcohol
or
2 Grains of Ambergris Well Rubbed in 2 Ounces of Sugar
8 Ounces Acetic Ether

Manufacture of Liquors, 1853

250
Old Roanoke Whiskey
(About 40 Gallons)

35 Gallons Distilled 80 to 90 Proof Whiskey
3 Gallons Honey Dissolved in 2 Gallons of Water

1 Quart Decoction of Strong Tea
8 Ounces Bruised Bitter Almonds
6 Drops Creosote
10 Drops Oil of Wintergreen Dissolved in 1 Ounce of
   Alcohol

The bitter almonds give to this whiskey that peculiar nutty
flavor on which its celebrity rests.

Manufacture of Liquors, 1853

251
Old Rye Whiskey
(5 Gallons)

4 Gallons 80 to 140 Proof Alcohol
1 Gallon Alcoholic Solution of Starch
1 Pint Decoction of Tea
1 Pint Infusion of Almonds
1 Ounce Tincture of Cochineal
4 Ounces Burnt Sugar
3 Drops Oil of Wintergreen Dissolved in 1 Ounce Alcohol

By some, rye whiskey is colored only of a slight brownish
tinge, with burnt sugar alone.

Manufacture of Liquors, 1853

252
Old Rye Whiskey
(About 125 Gallons)

100 Gallons Distilled 80 to 90 Proof Whiskey
20 Gallons Water
5 Gallons Honey
25 Drops Wintergreen Dissolved in 10 Ounces Alcohol
5 Ounces Acetic Ether
1 Pint Tincture Sanders
1 Pint Burnt Sugar Coloring

Manufacture of Liquors, 1853

253
Scotch Whiskey
(About 136 Gallons)

92 Gallons 80 to 140 Proof Alcohol
35 Gallons Water
6 Gallons Honey Dissolved in 3 Gallons Water
50 Drops Creosote
Burnt Sugar for Color

Manufacture of Liquors, 1853

254
Cheap Scotch Whiskey
(About 40 Gallons)

30 Gallons Distilled 80 to 90 Proof Whiskey
35 Pounds Sugar Dissolved in 8 Gallons Water
3 Quarts Strong Tea
1 Quart Tincture Grains of Paradise
1 Pint Tincture of Sanders Coloring
1 Pint Burnt Sugar Coloring
10 Drops Creosote

Manufacture of Liquors, 1853

255
Tuscaloosa Whiskey
(About 107 Gallons)

100 Gallons Distilled 80 to 90 Proof Whiskey
4 Gallons Pale Ale
3 Gallons Jamaica Rum

This should be colored very slight, as the spirit used may
contain sufficient coloring for the whole. This whiskey
usually comes in half-barrels, and stands deservedly high
with consumers; as yet it only has a local reputation.

Manufacture of Liquors, 1853

256
Champagne
(About 65 Gallons)

60 Gallons Cider
3 Gallons 80 to 140 Proof Alcohol
2-$\frac{1}{2}$ Gallons Honey

Boil and ferment the above; fine [settle out the impurities] with three pints boiling milk.

Manufacture of Liquors, 1853

257
Red Wine
(About 125 Gallons)

3 Bushels of Turnips or Beets
125 Gallons Water
1 Peck Radishes

Ferment the above until pleasantly sour to the taste, then adjust with honey and coloring. Turnips are preferable to beets, as beets leave a somewhat unpleasant taste, though sugar, aromatics and spirit will conceal it. A very fine champagne is prepared from fermented turnips and radishes...

Manufacture of Liquors, 1853

258
Cheap White Wine
(About 108 Gallons)

100 Gallons Clear Soft Water
8 Gallons Honey
3 Pints Yeast

Keep in a warm place in the sun until fermentation causes a pleasant acidity to the taste, then add

5 Ounces Bruised Bitter Almonds
4 Gallons 80 to 140 Proof Alcohol
4 Ounces Ground Mustard
5 Gallons Tincture of Grains of Paradise
6 Ounces Horseradish

Allow the mass to stand for four days, and then add three pints of boiling milk.

Manufacture of Liquors, 1853

259
Port Wine
(About 124 Gallons)

100 Gallons Claret
12 Gallons 80 to 140 Proof Alcohol
12 Gallons Honey
1 Pound Red Tartar
12 Ounces Powdered Catechu
1 Pint Wheat Paste
2 Ounces Bruised Ginger
2 Ounces Cassia
1 Pint Tincture of Orris Root
6 Ounces Bruised Cochineal in 1 Gallon of the Above Spirit
1 Pint Burnt Sugar Coloring

Adjust the strength with Tincture of Grains of Paradise and decoction of tea.

Manufacture of Liquors, 1853

Temperance Drinks

Harper's 1874 "Bottle Imp" illustration expressed the temperance viewpoint on the evils of liquor.

Not everyone wanted the high-proof wonders of the day. Many who had imbibed too much "made the pledge" and requested nonalcoholic drinks. To please those who remained dry, bartenders and amateur mixologists reached into their bag of tricks and brought forth drinks suitable for abstinence or recovery.

260
Drink for the Dog Days

A bottle of soda water poured into a large goblet, in which a lemon ice has been placed, forms a deliciously cool and refreshing drink. But it should be taken with some care, and positively avoided while you are very hot.

Bon-Vivant's Companion, 1862

261
Jersey Cocktail

2 Dashes Bitters
Apple Cider
1 Teaspoonful Powdered Sugar or Rock Candy
Lemon Peel

Dissolve the sugar with the bitters in a tumbler, fill one-third full of shaved ice, and the balance with cider. Shake well, and serve with lemon peel on the top.

Bon-Vivant's Companion, 1862
Gentleman's Table Guide, 1873

262
Nectar

1 Dram Citric Acid
1 Scruple Bicarbonate of Potash
1 Ounce White Sugar

Fill a soda water bottle nearly full of water, drop in the potash and sugar, and lastly the citric acid. Cork the bottle up immediately, and shake. As soon as the crystals are dissolved, the nectar is fit for use. It may be colored with a small portion of cochineal.

Bon-Vivant's Companion, 1862

263
Soda Cocktail

2 Dashes Bitters
Soda
1 Teaspoonful Powdered Sugar or Rock Candy
Lemon Peel

Dissolve the sugar with the bitters in a tumbler, fill one-third full of shaved ice, and the balance with cider. Shake well, and serve with lemon peel on the top.

Bon-Vivant's Companion, 1862

Glossary

Sampling and bottling area at Werner & Company's "champagne depot" in New York City. Champagne was a popular ingredient in mixed drinks and punches. It was not uncommon for liquor manufacturers to have areas for customers to taste their wares.

Absinthe

A potent 136 proof, licorice-flavored, anise-based spirit developed in the 18th century and banned in most countries since 1915. It contained wormwood and poisonous combinations of herbs that created epileptic and stupefying conditions in heavy drinkers. It was either diluted 50/50 with water in special drip-glasses, or added to mixed drinks.

Weaker anise based liquors, without the harmful ingredients and high-proof, may be substituted for absinthe. *Pernod*, a 90 proof anise liquor made by an old French absinthe firm, is recommended. Despite the health risk absinthe has had a recent comeback in Japan.

Acetic Acid

The essential sour element in vinegar. For the squeamish, Pierre Lacour recommended substituting 1 quart vinegar for 1 ounce acetic acid or sulfuric acid.

Acetic Ether

A distillate of acetic acid, sulfuric acid and alcohol that Pierre Lacour used as an early flavor enhancer. He found its taste so pleasant he advised using it to produce fraudulent whiskeys, brandies and cordials.

Aerated Lemonade

Imported British bottled lemonade made effervescent with carbonated water. A credible imitation can be made by mixing unflavored seltzer water with lemonade.

Alcohol

Always grain alcohol, never wood alcohol, which is poisonous. In the 1860s, proof spirit was 92% pure alcohol and 8% water, grain oil (fusel oil) and other matter. Proper whiskey contained 40% proof spirit (80 proof). If a barrel of whiskey was tested, and found to be "below proof," an appropriate amount of 82.5% alcohol was added to raise the alcohol content to 40% proof spirit. In the 1860s, as today, alcohol was usually filtered to remove grain oils and other impurities that added bitterness or undesired flavors.

When recipes call for pure alcohol, use 195 Proof (97.5% alcohol) *Everclear* diluted with water to the proper strength. Only individuals who wish to become candidates for liver transplants drink *Everclear* straight.

Alcoholic Solution of Starch

A mixture of starch and alcohol used to give body to fraudulent whiskey.

Ale

Ale is made from malt, or malt and cereal grains, hops and water. It tends to be more aromatic and bitter than beer because of the malt. Ale was not regarded to be as sensitive to heat and travel as beer and was shipped in the bottle for long distances. Bitter Ale had considerably more hops added to it and Old Ale was aged various lengths of time. Scotch Ale was imported from Scotland and was historically believed, like the Scotch, to be a strong, hardy ale.

Aloe

The American century plant. Pierre Lacour referred to the African aloe, which had a purgative effect that simulated strength in fraudulent liquors.

Alum

A double sulfate of aluminum and potassium having strong astringent qualities. Used in fraudulent liquors, in perilous quantities, to simulate strength.

Ambergris

A cloudy, dark, morbid secretion of the sperm whale used by the perfume industry. Because it becomes pleasingly fragrant upon heating, some bartenders used it in hot punches and mixed drinks. It is expensive and potent.

Amourette

Identical to modern Amaretto.

Angelic Essence

A concentrated solution of alcohol and the roots of the angelica plant. The angelica plant is native to Europe and Asia. Its roots are sometimes called the "roots of the Holy Ghost" because they contain fragrant oils used in perfume and as a tonic. Recommended by Pierre Lacour as a means of providing fragrance in fraudulent cordials.

Angelica Wine

A sweet, fruity California dessert wine produced from Mission grapes.

Angostura Bitters - See Bitters

Applejack - See Brandy

Aromatic Tincture

A flavoring popular between 1850-80 used in mixed drinks and punches. Jerry Thomas' recipe was:

Take of ginger, cinnamon, orange peel, each one ounce; valerian half an ounce, alcohol two quarts, macerate [soak] in a closed vessel for fourteen days, then filter through unsized paper.

Valerian is an herb with white or pink flowers and a medicinal root. A drug made from its root is used as a sedative and an antispasmodic.

Arrack, Batavia (now spelled Arak)

The term *arrack* is derived from the Arabic word for "juice" or "sweat." It is a generic term simply meaning "spirits." Beverages called *arrack, arak* or *raki* were brewed in the Indies, East Indies and Middle East. However, the drinks of the Civil War era were made with Batavia Arrack.

Batavia arrack (sometimes spelled arak) is a rum produced from molasses that comes from the sugar factories near Batavia, on the island of Java, Indonesia. Because of the special treatment given to the molasses and the special quality of the river water used in fermentation, a dry, highly aromatic rum results. The quality of arrack owes much to the wild, uncultured yeast *Saccharomyces vordermanni* and to the little cakes of specially cooked and dried red Javanese rice that are placed in the fermenting tubs of molasses.

The arak is aged for three or four years in Java, after which it is shipped to Holland where it is aged for another four to six years, blended, and then bottled.

Arak is a brandy like rum of great pugnancy and rumminess and is used as is any other rum. In Sweden, however, its greatest use is for making Swedish Punsch. (Harold Grossman. *Grossman's Guide to Wines, Beers, and Spirits.* New York: Charles Scribner's Sons, 1977.)

Popular in Europe, arrack is difficult to obtain in the United States. Dark rum may be substituted in drinks calling for Batavia Arrack.

Balm

A weedy, perennial herb native to the Mediterranean which tastes like lemon and smells like mint. In the 1860s, balm was used to treat headaches, asthma, fever, spasms, and flatulence. The oil was used in salves for healing wounds and was distilled as a perfume. Fresh sprigs of balm were put into wine or other drinks to give them "quickness."

Batavia Arrack - See Arrack

Beer

The majority of pre-1890 beers were lagered (cellered) beers brewed from malt, cereal grains, hops and water. Refrigerated railroad cars were not in common use prior to the 1890s, and pasteurization was considered detrimental to the taste of beer, so few brands were shipped long distances. Instead, major brewers such as Anheuser-Busch formed cooperatives and sold supplies and their special yeast strains across the country. End quality of the beer varied greatly according the skill of the brewmaster, usually a German immigrant. Any quality lager beer made with 100% natural ingredients may be used in the recipes—avoid light beers.

Bitter Ale - See Ale

Bitters

Aromatic oils and essences from fruits, herbs, plants, seeds, etc. in an alcohol base used to impart a bitter flavor to drinks. The most widely distributed in the 1860s were Angostura, Bogart's and Boker's bitters. Angostura Bitters is the sole 1860s brand still commonly available. It is made with gentian and vegetable extracts and was first compounded in Angostura, Venezuela, about 1830. Peychaud's bitters, made in New Orleans, was not registered until 1886.

Boker's Bitters

A popular old bitter apparently no longer available. Substitute Angostura bitters.

Borage

An annual herb, native to Europe and North Africa, with a cucumber-like taste. The flowers and leafy tops were steeped in drinks of British origin such as punches, cups and negus.

Bourbon Whiskey - See Whiskey

Brandy

Liquor distilled from grape wine or a mash of fruit and fruit nuts or seeds. Liqueurs are flavored with real or artificial ingredients but are usually not distilled. Major types include:

Applejack, also called hard cider, is distilled from apples and of American origin. It was used as a mixer in cocktails, fancy drinks and punches. Still commonly available and growing in popularity.

Brandy is a spirit distilled from a fermented mash of fruit, or wine, and manufactured from a wide variety of fruits in several parts of the world.

Cognac is brandy distilled from the wine of grapes grown mainly in the Charente and Charente-Maritime departments of France. It comes in several grades and can be aged for twenty years or more.

Fruit Brandies include *Applejack* and *Abricotine, Blackberry Brandy, Kirschwasser, Cherry Brandy* and others. They are frequently among the most difficult liquors to find and should not be confused with liqueurs.

True fruit brandies contain only the distilled essences of the fruit, whereas Cremes and liqueurs such as Benedictine contain mixed ingredients and added sugar syrup. Flavored brandies, containing grape brandy and fruit essences, may be substituted, as long as they are made with true fruit and not synthetic flavorings. However, they are usually sweeter and may not give a true impression of the original drinks.

Burgundy Wine

Dry wines, predominantly red, from the French departments of Cote d'Or, Yonne, Saone-et-Loire and the arrondissement of Villefranchae-sur-Saone. The best red wines are produced from Pinot Noir and Gamay grapes while the white wines are from Chardonnay grapes. So called "California burgundies" may have the characteristics of French burgundies but should not be substituted.

Burnt Sugar Coloring

A dark coloring added to imitation liquors. It was made by heating sugar over a fire for an hour and a half, adding an equal quantity of water, and straining the mixture.

Butyric Ether

A flavoring with a strong odor of pineapples made from distilled rancid butter and sulfuric acid. Pierre Lacour gave recipes for fraudulent champagne and brandies using butyric ether. He advised that its strong odor would mask impurities, such as grain oil, in cheap alcohol.

Calf's Foot Jelly or Calves Foot Jelly

Gelatin obtained by boiling the hooves of cattle in water. Any unflavored gelatin may be used in recipes.

California Claret Wine - See Claret Wine

Capillaire

Originally a sweet syrup made with the maidenhair fern known as early as 1754. By the Civil War it was an orange-flavored sweetener made by stirring one wine glass (two ounces) of Curacao (use modern Cointreau liqueur) into a pint of simple sugar syrup. Usually kept on the back bar in a corked bottle ready for use.

Catawba Wine

Dry and sweet Catawba wines gained favor in the 19th century due to the efforts of vintner Nicholas Longworth of Cincinnati, Ohio. His cultivation of the Catawba grape led to sales of over 100,000 bottles a year. Today, Catawba, Isabella, and Delaware grapes are the primary constituents in sparkling champagnes made in the eastern U.S. Some sparkling Catawba wine is made in limited quantities; if unavailable, substitute dry or sweet champagne from Ohio or New York.

Catechu

The astringent bark of two East Indian acacia plants. Pierre Lacour recommended it as an ingredient to simulate strength in fraudulent liquors because it constricted the throat.

Champagne

Famous sparkling wines imported from the Champagne district in northern France made from red and white Pinot Noir, Chardonnay and Pinot Meunier grapes. Champagne was considered a luxury item and a sign of civilization. It was packed to some of the most remote areas of the American West as early as the 1850s; where whiskey arrived, champagne was not far behind. Although champagne was available in the full range of very dry to sweet, sweet varieties were probably more common. Mumms was a leading imported "true" champagne, while numerous New York, Ohio and California vineyards produced domestic varieties.

Chartreuse

A brandy-based French liqueur developed in the 18th century distilled and blended from more than 130 herbs and spices. Available in yellow (80-86 proof) and the more common green (110 proof) versions.

Cherry Brandy

A dry 60 to 70 proof brandy distilled from fermented cherries. Kirschwasser is the common modern name for old-style cherry brandy. Cherry-flavored brandies should not be substituted; they are usually a mixture of diluted grain alcohol and imitation cherry flavoring.

Cherry Ice

Crushed ice flavored with cherry syrup used as an ingredient in some British drinks.

Cherry Syrup

Sugar syrup flavored with cherry extract, available in some groceries and delicatessens. Originally available in alcoholic and nonalcoholic versions. An 1862 recipe called for five gallons of fermented cherry juice and eighty pounds of sugar boiled together, skimmed, strained and bottled.

Cider, Hard - See Brandy

Citric Acid

"[The] peculiar acid to which limes and lemons owe their acidity; it is present also in the juice of other fruits, such as the cranberry, the red whortleberry, red gooseberry, currant, strawberry, raspberry, etc., etc. Citric acid is prepared from the juice of the lime or the lemon."

Manufacture of Liquors, 1853

Cinnamon Water - See Creme De Canelle

Claret Wine

English term for red wines from the Bordeaux region of France, usually fermented for a very short period and not aged. These wines were known in France by their uncorrupted name, Clairet, and are again being bottled under that name to separate them from aged Clarets. In the last century some Clarets were made by blending red and white wines from Bordeaux, a procedure now illegal under French law.

Cochineal - See Tincture of Cochineal

Cognac Brandy - See Brandy

Colorings

Imitation liquors featured a variety of colorings: caramel; brown sugar; bunt sugar; red sanders wood (see Sanders Wood); gamboge, a yellow resin from certain Thai and Cambodian trees; alkanet root, a European member of the borage family that yields a reddish-brown dye; logwood, the brownish-red heartwood of a Central American and West Indian tree; red beets; indigo, a blue plant dye used for coloring cordials; cochineal (see Tincture of Cochineal) an intensely red coloring made from the dried bodies of female cactus bugs.

Creme De Canelle

French cinnamon liqueur.

Creme De Noyau (also Noyaux)
Almond-flavored 50-60 proof liqueur made from the almonds and/or the pits of apricots, plums, peaches and cherries.

Creme De Vanilla
A 60 proof liqueur produced from Mexican or Caribbean vanilla beans.

Cream of Tartar
Purified and crystallized potassium bitartrate used in baking. Commonly available in grocery stores.

Creosote
Many of Pierre Lacour's fraudulent liquor recipes called for creosote, also called oil of tar. Ingesting concentrated creosote is dangerous, and some have even suggested that it is a carcinogen. Lacour said:

> Creosote or oil of tar is used for flavoring malt whiskey, or well cleaned corn whiskey, in imitation of Irish or Scotch whiskeys; from sixty to eighty drops in 100 gallons. Some contend that the addition of from thirty to fifty drops of cedar oil...perfects the imitation. It is not an unusual occurrence to find a large portion of this whiskey made from common corn whiskey, with the grain oil concealed by the powerful odor of the creosote.
>
> *Manufacture of Liquors, 1853*

Curacao
Also spelled Curacoa, is a common 54-60 proof liqueur produced from orange peels. The best Curacao is made from the famous green oranges grown on scrubby trees found on the West Indian island of Curacao. Vegetable coloring is added to create red, blue and other versions. Cointreau is the modern brand name for 19th century Curacao.

Essence of Cloves - See Tincture of Cloves

Essence of Ginger
"Combine two pounds of ground ginger, six gallons of 95% alcohol, and four gallons of water. Macerate [soak] for two weeks, strain and filter."
Schultz, Manual for the Manufacture of Cordials, 1862

Essence of Peppermint
"Dissolve two ounces of oil of peppermint in six gallons of 95% alcohol. Add four gallons of water. Color with tincture of turmeric [use saffron-yellow food coloring] and filter."
Schultz, Manual for the Manufacture of Cordials, 1862

Gin

Gin was a 17th century Dutch invention originally intended as a medicine. The British became so enamored of the Juniper berry-flavored liquor that moralists felt bound to preach against widespread public over-indulgence. It was less popular in 19th century America, used primarily as an alternative to whiskey in mixed drinks.

Holland Gin, called Genever by the Dutch and quality liquor dealers, is distilled differently from British and American gins giving it a heavier, full bodied flavor. It is sold in distinctive crockery bottles by firms such as Bols.

Ginger Ale (Irish)

A mixture of carbonated water and extract of Jamaica ginger probably invented in Ireland. Bottled Irish Ginger Ale was an important mixer for many varieties of drinks.

Ginger Beer

A sparkling alcoholic drink and mixer of British or Irish origin made of fermented ginger, sugar, yeast, cream of tartar and water. It is bottled before fermentation is complete, resulting in the fizz of carbonic acid gas. Ginger beer is now produced in this country as a nonalcoholic soft drink; some specialty liquor stores carry the original alcoholic version.

Ginger Syrup

Mix seven-and-a-half ounces of simple syrup and half an ounce of the Essence of Ginger together.

Lacour, Manual on the Manufacture of Liquors, 1853

Grains of Paradise - See Tincture of Grains of Paradise

Grenadine Syrup

A red sweetener made from pomegranates and available in better delicatessens and groceries. May contain 2.5% alcohol.

Gum Syrup

A mixture of white gum arabic, sugar and water used as a sweetener in mixed drinks. Gum arabic is obtained from species of the acacia tree and is used to make glue (mucilage). Where gum syrup is called for, substitute Simple Syrup.

Hock Wine - See Hockheimer Wine

Hockheimer Wine

Also called Hock or Rhine wine is a sweet white wine produced from Riesling grapes in the Rheingau area of Germany between Hockheim and Lorch. These fruity and mellow vintages have been a favorite over the last hundred years.

Holland Gin - See Gin

Hops

The dried flower of the female hop vine. Hops are used to give brewed beverages bitterness and character. The finest hops come from Czechoslovakia, but they are also grown on the western seaboard of the U.S.

Hungarian Wine - See Tokay Wine

Irish Ginger Ale - See Ginger Ale

Irish Whiskey - See Whiskey

Isabella Wine

Pale rose-colored wine from a reddish-black native American grape. Much in favor in the 19th century, it is now grown primarily to be blended into sparkling wines. One current authority states that it is a somewhat bland wine based upon modern Swiss Isabella wines. Nondescript pale red wines may be substituted for Isabella.

Islay Whiskey - See Whiskey - Scotch Whiskey

Jamaica Rum - See Rum

Kirschwasser

A dry, 90 proof fruit brandy distilled from cherries and cherry pits. Not to be confused with sweet Maraschino liqueur. The best Kirsch came from the Black Forest area of Germany, Alsace and Switzerland. The cherry stones give true Kirschwasser its bitterness.

Loaf Sugar

Sugar shaped into small bricks or loaves, common in the last century. Bartenders crushed, ground or powdered whatever quantities were required in specific recipes. Substitute appropriate modern grinds of sugar.

Lump Sugar

The same as modern sugar cubes; hence the saying "one lump, or two?"

Madeira Wine

Fortified (brandy added) wines from the Portuguese islands of Madeira off the northwest coast of Africa. Aged in wooden casks under heat, some Madeira wines a century or more old are still available and vastly superior to aged Sherry. Use the sweeter dessert varieties in mixed drinks.

Malt

Roasted germinated grain, usually barley, used in brewing and distilling.

Maraschino Liqueur

A sweet, 80 proof cherry liqueur once made exclusively in the Dalmatia region of Yugoslavia. Now produced almost solely in Italy. Not to be confused with the dry *Kirschwasser* brandy.

Moselle Wine

German wine made largely from Riesling grapes which grow in the slatey soil along the banks of the Moselle River.

Oil of Cinnamon

A concentrated essence of cinnamon available at some groceries and specialty shops.

Oil of Juniper

An extract of juniper berries used to flavor real and fraudulent gin. A powerful diuretic.

Oil of Turpentine

A flavoring, having a vague similarity to oil of juniper, derived from the oleoresin (sap) of pine trees. It was used to flavor cheap gin and probably had adverse effects on the health. Strasburg oil of turpentine was said to have been the best.

Oil of Wine

A distillation of sulfuric acid, alcohol and potassa (potash and lime) used to fake the aroma of imported brandies.

Old Ale - See Ale

Orange Brandy

Brandy distilled from oranges is seldom called for; normally the liqueur Curacao (available under the brand name Cointreau) is favored in its place. Imitation orange brandies were made by flavoring grain alcohol with orange and other oils.

A palatable orange-flavored brandy may be made by placing a gallon of good brandy or Cognac, the thinly sliced rinds of nine oranges and two lemons, and two pounds of sugar in a tightly sealed stoneware crock. Allow to stand for a month, shaking daily for ten minutes. Then bottle and seal.

Jerry Thomas, The Bon-Vivant's Companion, 1862

Orange Flower Water

An extract of orange flowers, orange peel, water (and sometimes alcohol) used for flavoring. Commonly available in delicatessens and grocery stores.

Oranges - (Seville, China, Blood)

Three types of oranges were called for in recipe books of the 1860s: Blood, Seville and China. Blood and China oranges were sweet, Seville oranges were sour.

Orgeat Syrup

Sugar syrup flavored with almond extract, available in some groceries and delicatessens.

Orris Root

A native plant of Italy and South Europe having an odor of violets and an acrid, bitter taste. Pierre Lacour soaked eight ounces of orris root in a gallon of alcohol for eight days and used it in fraudulent brandies, wines, cordials and gins.

Parfait Amour

Also Parfait d'Amour. The French name of this 50 proof liqueur means "Perfect Love." Produced from a variety of formulae, but usually including oranges, lemons, coriander seeds, vanilla, flowers and herbs. Common in 19th century taverns, but colored red then as opposed to the modern violet.

Bols, the only domestic producer of Parfait Amour, discontinued production in the 1980s. Some liquor dealers still have bottles tucked away, and a few larger establishments carry imported Parfait Amour. This 1862 formula for the liquor was used by bartenders in remote areas who had access to a still:

Grind eight ounces of cedrat rinds, four ounces of lemon peel and one-half ounce of cloves. Macerate for three hours in three gallons of 95% grain alcohol and three-and-a-half gallons of water. Distill three gallons of flavored alcohol from the water. Add thirty pounds of sugar dissolved in five and one-eighth gallons of water, and color deep red and filter.

Schultz, Manual for the Manufacture of Cordials, 1862

Peach Brandy

A 60 to 70 proof brandy distilled from fermented peaches. Peach-flavored liqueurs may be substituted, however look for the "true fruit" designation.

Peach Syrup

A rarely called for syrup made by adding peach juice to Simple Syrup. Many variations in quantities of syrup to juice exist.

Pellitory

An African plant, the root of which is used as an irritant. Used to fake strength in liquors. Pierre Lacour stated that:

> Its taste is peculiar, slight at first, but afterwards acidulous, saline, and acrid, attended with a burning and tingling sensation over the whole mouth and throat, which continues for some time, and excites a copious flow of saliva.
>
> *Manufacture of Liquors, 1853*

Pineapple Syrup

Pineapple syrup continues to be made for "tropical" style drinks. An old recipe called for boiling one-and-a-half pounds of pineapple juice with two pounds of sugar until a syrup formed.

Pineapple Oil

Grate 4 pounds of pineapple, soak in 4 gallons of 190 proof alcohol for one week. Filter the solution through cloth. Add it to a simple syrup made from 48 pounds of sugar boiled for three hours with three gallons of water. Skim, mix and filter if necessary.

Manual for the Manufacture of Cordials, 1862

Plain Syrup - See Simple Syrup

Port Wine

Sweet fortified wines from the Douro region of Portugal. Several grades of Port are made, but most are not considered worthy of drinking unless at least fifteen to twenty years old. Modern, unaged blended ports and white ports were not served in the last century.

Porter

Bitter tasting member of the beer and ale family made from charred malt, which gives it a dark brown appearance. It is regarded as the forerunner of stout. Not to be confused with Port wine.

Prune Spirit

This concentrate was used by Pierre Lacour in the production of several fraudulent liquors. His recipe called for soaking any quantity of prunes in twice their mass of 80% alcohol for ten days, then adding an equal quantity of Jamaica rum.

Raspberry Liqueur

A 50-60 proof liqueur, originating in France, manufactured either from expensive wild or cheaper cultivated raspberries. Chambord is the best known imported brand.

Raspberry Syrup

Available in delicatessens and some grocery stores.

Ferment 5 gallons of raspberry juice for 2 days. Boil 80 pounds of sugar in the raspberry juice for 2 minutes or until it dissolves. When the mixture begins to boil and rise to the top of the pan, throw in a little cold water to prevent the sugar from running over.

You must let the sugar rise three times before commencing to skim it, each time cooling the mixture by the cold water just spoken of. The fourth time the sugar rises skim it completely, and drop the cold water gently in as occasion may require, continuing to take the scum off (which is rather white), until no more comes upon the surface. The syrup must now be strained through a fine sieve—one made of cloth or a flannel bag will do.

Manufacture of Cordials, 1862

Red Tartar - See Tartar, Cream of

Rhine Wine - See Hockheimer Wine

Rock Candy

Crushed and used as a sweetener in place of pulverized or granulated sugar.

Rum

Spirit made from the byproducts of sugarcane refining: molasses and the skimmings of boiled sugar. Most 19th century rum came either from St. Croix (also called Santa Cruz) in the Virgin Islands or from Jamaica. Lesser varieties included Batavia for Batavia Arrack, and Medford, after a city in Massachusetts. Medford became a generic name for rum distilled on the east coast of the U.S.

Rye Whiskey - See **Whiskey**

Sanders Wood, Red (Sandal Wood)
A coloring, recommended by Pierre Lacour, for imitation liquors:

The Preparation of Liquor Coloring Red Sanders Wood [Sandal Wood]—Red Sanders Wood comes in round or angular sticks, internally of a blood red color, and externally brown from exposure to the air; compact and heavy, of a fibrous texture; it is kept in the shops in the state of small chips, raspings, or coarse powder. It has but little smell or taste, and imparts a red color to alcohol, ether, and alkaline solutions, but not to water. Coloring is obtained from Sanders Wood, in the proportion of one pound of the wood to one gallon of proof spirit, and allowed to stand for twenty-four hours, and then drawn off and filtered through sand, to the depth of twelve to fourteen inches. The Sanders Wood should be subjected to the action of the spirit as long as it continues to yield any color. This color is used for brandies, combined with burnt sugar, also for coloring cherry bounce, wines, &c.

Manufacture of Liquors, 1853

Santa Cruz Rum - See **Rum**

Sauterne Wine
Naturally sweet white wine made in the Sauternes district of France from Semillon and Sauvignon grapes. Harvesting takes place in the autumn after the grapes have over-ripened and a beneficial mold has formed.

Scotch Ale - See **Ale**

Scotch Whiskey - See **Whiskey**

Seltzer Water
Naturally or artificially effervescent mineral water containing small quantities of salt sodium, calcium, and magnesium carbonates. This term is frequently used interchangeably with soda water, mineral water, Appollinaris water, and Vichy water. Mineral waters are usually natural carbonated waters, such as Apollinaris, whereas, soda waters are artificially carbonated.

Sherry
Spanish fortified wine with an alcoholic content of 16% to 18% made predominantly from the Palamino grape. Grape brandy is added to increase

its alcoholic content. The two main types of Sherry are the *Fino Amontillado* and *Oloroso*.

Brown Sherry is a very dark, sweet wine similar to Creme Sherry. It is popular in England and Scotland, but not the United States. Substitute Harvey's Bristol Cream.

Simple Syrup
"Add two and a half pounds of refined sugar to one pint of water, dissolve the sugar over heat, and remove the scum. Strain the solution, while hot, through a flannel bag."

The Manufacture of Liquor, 1853

Solferino
Purplish pink dye made from aniline and orthotoluidine, commonly used as food coloring from the 1860s to the 1890s. Substitute modern food coloring.

Sparkling Wine
Effervescent wines made by either the champagne method or by adding carbon dioxide directly to the wine. Examples: champagne, spumanti and sparkling catawba.

Spirit of Vanilla
An antiquated term for Vanilla extract.

St. Croix Rum - See Rum

Stout
Strong porter, originally known as "extra stout" porter and made in Britain.

Strawberry Syrup
Common flavoring for mixed drinks. An 1853 recipe directed bartenders to make it with one pint of strained strawberry juice, two-and-a-half pounds of sugar, and half a glass of alcohol. Dissolve the sugar in the strawberry juice over a gentle heat and set aside for 24 hours. Then remove the scum, pour off the clear liquor from the dregs, and add the alcohol.

Sulfuric Acid
Sulfuric acid, used by Pierre Lacour in many vile fraudulent liquor recipes. Sulfuric acid, astringent pellitory, and pepper were added to give fake liquors their burning sensation.

In the 1860s, sulfuric acid was produced by burning sulfur, combined with one-eighth its weight in nitre, in a sealed lead chamber. Commercial sulfuric acid had a specific gravity of 1.8433 and contained 22% water. It was shipped in wicker-covered green glass demijohns (large bottles) called carboys. Much commercially produced sulfuric acid also contained arsenic, although this was of little concern to charlatans in the liquor trade.

If the inexperienced liquor "manufacturer" did not want to risk chemical burns, or dead customers, Lacour recommended substituting 1 quart of vinegar when recipes called for 1 ounce of sulfuric acid.

Sulfuric Ether

An acidic liquid with a sweet odor and hot taste distilled from sulfuric acid and alcohol. One of Pierre Lacour's ingredients in spurious rum and brandies.

Tartar (Cream of, Red)

Purified and crystallized potassium bitartrate used in baking. Plain tartar, is a partially purified product. The composition of red tartar is uncertain.

Tincture of Capsicum

Capsicum is the genus name for the hot pepper family. Tincture of capsicum is a concentrated solution of chili, Cayenne or red pepper that was used in fake liquors to give them a burning taste. We suggest using any type of Louisiana hot sauce, such as McIlhenny Co. Tabasco pepper sauce.

Tincture of Cochineal

A brilliant red coloring made from the dried bodies of female cactus bugs. Pierre Lacour manufactured it by boiling an ounce of cochineal in a quart of water with tartar, salt of tartar, and alum.

Tincture of Grains of Paradise

Description and Preparation of Pepper, Known Under the Name of Grains of Paradise—Guinea pepper, and Melegueta pepper, are kept in the shops; small seeds, of a round or ovate form, often angular, minutely rough, brown externally, white within, of a feebly aromatic odor when rubbed between the fingers, and of a strong, hot, and peppery taste. They are brought from Guinea; their effects on the system are analogous to those of pepper.

Guinea pepper is prepared for use by grinding, or pulverizing to a powder, one to one and a half pound of the powder to a gallon of proof spirit, and used for giving false strength to liquor, in the proportion of from one to two quarts, to forty gallons; this tincture should be well strained to prevent muddiness in the barrel, after the pepper has been added.

The burning sensation produced by pepper and alcohol is nearly identical; and it must be obvious that the former will answer all the purposes of the latter, with the exception of not furnishing the intoxicating quality, which must be added in the form of alcohol. In the manufacture of all the cheap light wines, cordials, &c. where alcohol would be an important consideration, pecuniarily, Guinea pepper will answer admirably.

Manufacture of Liquors, 1853

Tincture of Mustard

A concentrated solution of acrid black mustard seed and water used to provide false strength to fraudulent imitation liquors.

Tokay Wine

Commonly called Hungarian Wine, it was difficult to obtain after the Civil War because of damage to the vines by the vine louse phylloxera in 1875 and fungus in 1891. The vineyards were rebuilt on American vine stock resistant to phylloxera and by 1900 mixed drink recipes were again calling for the use of Tokay or Hungarian wine.

Triple Sec

Originally a proprietary name for Curacao. The original 19th century formulation of Curacao is still available under the brand name Cointreau.

Turpentine - See Oil of Turpentine

Vanilla Cordial - See Creme De Vanilla

Vichy Water - See Seltzer Water

Whiskey

Whiskey was by far the most popular 19th century American liquor, far outstripping Brandy, Rum, Applejack and Gin. Crude whiskey was made on the frontier as soon as the materials for stills became available or the ingredients for imitation whiskey could be secured. Tastes for whiskey improved as towns became established—cheap Rye was replaced by Bourbon and imported Irish and Scotch whiskies.

Bourbon Whiskey originated in Bourbon County, Kentucky in 1789, where the first was produced by Reverend Elijah Craig. It is sweeter and more full bodied than Scotch or Irish whiskey, and is usually not blended. Made from a minimum of 51 percent corn plus rye and malt, it has a proof not more than 160, and is stored in charred white oak barrels for at least two years.

The charred oak barrels give Bourbon its distinctive taste. Water is added at bottling to reduce the proof, but never below 80. Bourbon and Rye Whiskey were the two most popular 19th century American whiskeys.

Canadian Whiskey is produced from cereal grain and noted for its lightness in comparison to Scotch, Rye and Bourbon. Its popularity in American saloons dates from around 1900.

Irish Whiskey—Usque-baugh is the original Irish name for whiskey and it has been made in the Emerald Isle since at least the 10th century. Irish whiskey is made from a mash of malted and unmalted barley, rye, oats and wheat. Unlike Scotch whiskey, the malted barley in Irish whiskey is not dried over a peat fire and therefore lacks the smokey flavor of Scotch. Additionally, Irish whiskey is distilled three times, as opposed to twice for Scotch, and is aged a minimum of five years, as opposed to three years for Scotch.

Rye Whiskey and *Bourbon*, were the two most common whiskies in American saloons. Rye whiskey is a distilled spirit, not exceeding 160 proof, made from a grain mash containing at least 51% rye, and aged at least two years.

Scotch Whiskey is now usually a blend of several Scotch malt whiskies derived from barley. The process of blending Scotch whiskey to attain the best mixture became widespread during the 1870s, and now it is difficult to find a straight Scotch whiskey. Each Scotch is aged for a minimum of three years in oak casks. It is probably safe to assume that Scotch whiskies called for in recipes of the 1860s and later were unblended.

Islay whiskey is a straight malt Scotch whiskey.

White Tokay Wine - See Tokay Wine

Yeast
A single-celled microscopic plant that changes sugars in brewed beverages into alcohol. The character of the beverage is defined by the yeast and its purity.

Selected Bibliography

Bartenders', Gentlemens', and Distillers' Guides

_____. *Barkeeper's Ready Reference*. St. Louis: A.V. Beville, 1871.

Chase, A.W. *Dr. Chase's Recipes*. Ann Arbor: A.W. Chase, 1867.

Haney, Jessie. *Haney's Steward and Barkeeper's Manual*. New York: J. Haney & Co., 1869.

Lacour, Pierre. *The Manufacture of Liquors, Wines, and Cordials, Without the Aid of Distillation*. New York: Dick and Fitzgerald, 1853.

Monzert, Leonard. *The Independent Liquorist*. New York: Dick and Fitzgerald, c. 1866.

Newton, Addison V. *The Saloon Keeper's Companion...* Worcester: West & Lee, 1875.

Ricket, Edward. *The Gentleman's Table Guide and Table Companion*. London: F. Warne, 1873.

Roberts, George Edwin. *Cups and Their Customs*. London: John Van Voorst, 1863, 1869.

Schultz, Christian. *Manual for the Manufacture of Cordials, Liquors, Fancy Syrups, &c. &c.* New York: Dick and Fitzgerald, 1862.

Terrington, William. *Cooling Cups and Dainty Drinks*. London and New York: George Routledge and Sons, 1869.

Thomas, Jerry. *How to Mix Drinks, or the Bon-Vivant's Companion*. New York: Dick and Fitzgerald, 1862.

Other Sources

Ade, George. *The Old-Time Saloon*. New York: Ray Long and Richard R. Smith, Inc., 1931.

Asbury, Herbert. *The Bon-Vivant's Companion or How to Mix Drinks* by Jerry Thomas. New York: Grosset and Dunlap, 1934. [Reprint of 1862 edition of The Bon-Vivant's Companion with biographical notes on Jerry Thomas.]

Baron, Stanley. *Brewed in America*. Boston: Little, Brown and Co., 1962.

Beveridge, N.E., pseud. [Harold L. Peterson]. *Cups of Valor*. Harrisburg, PA: Stackpole Books, 1968.

Brown, James Hull. *Early American Beverages*. New York: Bonanza Books, 1966.

Carson, Gerald. *A Social History of Bourbon*. New York: Dodd, Mead and Co., 1963.

Cobb, Irvin S. *Red Likker*. New York: Cosmopolitan Book Co., 1929.

Dial, Scott. *Saloons of Denver*. Ft. Collins: The Old Army Press, 1973.

Edmunds, Lowell. *The Silver Bullet: The Martini in American Civilization*. Westport: Greenwood Press, 1981.

Efron, Vera, Mark Keller. *Selected Statistical Tables on the Consumption of Alcohol, 1850-1960*. New Brunswick, N.J.: Publications Division Rutgers Center of Alcohol Studies, 1963.

Emerson, Edward R. *Beverages Past and Present*. New York: G.P. Putnam's Sons, 1908.

Field, S.S. *The American Drink Book*. New York: Farer, Straus & Young, 1953.

Fox, Helen Morgenthau. *Gardening with Herbs for Flavor and Fragrance*. New York: Sterling Publishing Co., Inc., 1970.

Grossman, Harold J. *Grossman's Guide to Wines, Beers and Spirits*. New York: Charles Scribner's Sons, 1977.

Harwell, Richard Barksdale. *The Mint Julep*. Charlottesville: University Press of Virginia, 1975.

Hewitt, Edward, W.F. Axton. *Convivial Dickens: The Drinks of Dickens and his Times*. Athens: Ohio University Press, 1983.

Holmes, Jack D. L. *New Orleans Drinks and How to Mix Them.* New Orleans: Hope Publications, 1973.

Jackson, Michael. *The World Guide to Beer.* Philadelphia: Running Press, 1977.

Johnson, Byron A. and Sharon Peregrine Johnson. *The Wild West Bartenders' Guide: Saloonkeeping in the American West 1862-1905.* Texas Monthly Press, 1986.

Lichine, Alexis. *Alexis Lichine's New Encyclopedia of Wines and Spirits.* New York: Alfred A. Knopf, 1984.

Lord, Tony. *The World Guide to Spirits, Apertifs and Cocktails.* New York: Soverign Books, 1979.

Marshall, Jim. *The Swinging Doors.* Seattle: Frank McCaffrey Publishers, 1949.

Martin, Frederick. *An Encyclopedia of Drink and Drinking.* Toronto: Coles Publishing Co. Ltd., 1978.

Munsey, Cecil. *The Illustrated Guide to Collecting Bottles.* New York: Hawthorn Books, Inc., 1970.

Noling, A. W. *Beverage Literature: A Bibliography.* Metuchen, N.J.: Scarecrow Press, 1971.

Index to Drinks

(Paginated)

"Good Night" was the fifth and last of the Skinner series. All good celebrations had to come to an end, and hopefully with a safe return to camp. (William Welling)